The Communication Internship

Principles and Practices

Third Edition

Kory Floyd
Arizona State University

Michele Hammers
Loyola Marymount University

Clifton Scott
University of North Carolina, Charlotte

KENDALL/HUNT PUBLISHING COMPANY
4050 Westmark Drive   Dubuque, Iowa 52002

Contents

List of Figures

S O YOU'RE INTERESTED IN BECOMING AN INTERN? Congratulations! Doing an internship is one of the best ways for college students to gain practical working experience while also earning credit toward their degrees. And the communication field is *filled* with internship opportunities, from writing press releases to designing a corporate promotion to teaching English as a second language. Whatever your specific interests, chances are that an internship opportunity exists for you. But, how do you get started? Where do you find the right internship? What should you expect when you begin? These and many other questions are common for prospective interns to have. If you're unsure about these things, then this book is for you!

We have designed this book with practicality in mind. We begin in Chapter One by discussing what an internship is and by giving you some ideas about how to find the right internship for you. In Chapter Two we address the roles and responsibilities of the several people who will play a part in making your internship successful, and we give you an introduction to the laws and regulations that apply to your internship work. We know that your first days at an internship can be overwhelming, so in Chapter Three we tell you about what to expect and what you will need to keep in mind. In Chapter Four we discuss the role of your mentor, how to understand his or her expectations, and some ways to resolve conflict.

To help you succeed at your internship and in your future employment, we give you several tips in Chapter Five about professional development. Here, we address things like appropriate dress and self-presentation, time management, and group dynamics. Chapter Six is dedicated to professional writing and many of the things you need to keep in mind as you write memos or reports for your internship. In Chapter Seven, we discuss some of the more common problems that interns face at their worksites, from handling conflicts over hours or duties to dealing with workplace romance.

One of the most valuable tools you will have at your disposal as an intern will be your training in communication. In Chapter Eight we return to the topic of conflict and examine it in more detail. We'll discuss some of the communication strategies people use for managing conflict and we'll also talk about using conflict to your advantage. In Chapter Nine, we discuss your communication education and some of the ways it can inform your work. Finally, Chapter Ten addresses your post-collegiate job search. Here, we discuss the job search process and give you tips on resumes, cover letters, interviews, and negotiating job offers. There are several appendices at the end of the book. Most contain forms that you will need to complete your internship, while others provide examples of things that we discuss elsewhere in this book. We have perforated the book to make these appendices easy to pull out and use.

Our goal in preparing this book was to give you the tools to succeed at your internship and in your career. Of course, no single book can tell you everything you need to know. We realize that every student—and every internship—is different, and that the ideas and advice we offer will work better in some situations than in others. We hope, however, that by addressing some of the major principles of successful internships and by giving you some ideas of what to expect, we will help you to make your internship experience exactly what you want it to be.

Several people assisted in making this book possible. For their individual and collective contributions, we are most grateful to the faculty and staff of the Hugh Downs School of Human Communication at Arizona State University; the administration and staff of the College of Liberal Arts and Sciences at Arizona State University; and the editorial and production staff at Kendall/Hunt. Most of all, we are thankful for the many undergraduate and graduate students who do communication internships each year. It is to these students, and to their continued success, that we dedicate this text.

Kory Floyd, Michele Hammers, and Clifton Scott

Chapter One

An Introduction to Your Internship Experience

CONGRATULATIONS!

You have taken the first steps toward becoming a communication intern. You have chosen to undertake an experience that will be unlike any other you have encountered thus far. Internships provide excellent opportunities to apply your communication skills, gain practical knowledge in a field of interest to you, and help you prepare for the working world. Whether you have already begun work or are eagerly anticipating your first days on the job, the experiences and lessons that await you as a communication intern will be invaluable supplements to your undergraduate education.

The purpose of this book is to illuminate some of the many issues that are pertinent to your internship experience. We begin by discussing how you should select and finalize the details of your internship and what you should expect from your mentor, from the school, and from yourself. We then discuss issues surrounding your professional development that will be important not only for your internship but for your future employment success. We give you some examples of common problems that surface during internships and discuss ways to deal with them, and we address some of the ways in which your communication education applies to what you will do as an intern. Finally, we discuss the details of searching for employment after your internship, whether at your sponsoring organization or elsewhere.

As you work through this book, please keep in mind that internships vary almost as much as the students who occupy them. You may be working in a large corporation with formal procedures and policies, or in a small company with an informal, laid-back atmosphere. You may be one of several interns at your job site or you may be the only intern your organization has ever had. We realize that some of the issues we will discuss in this book will apply more to certain internship situations than to others. As you progress through the semester, we invite you to take the information, examples, and tips we provide in this book and filter them through your own experiences. In this way, we believe you will get the most out of this book, this class, and your internship. Good luck!

Purpose of an Internship Experience

YOU PROBABLY HAVE SEVERAL reasons why you decided to become an intern. Perhaps you want to gain hands-on experience working on a job that interests you. Maybe you are hoping to find full-time employment at your sponsoring organization. Or it may be that you have not had much work experience and feel you need some substance on your resume before you graduate. In truth, students take part in communication internships for a variety of reasons, and a good internship will provide students with a number of potential benefits.

The ideal internship is designed to benefit both the student and the sponsoring organization. It provides students with work experiences that they have not (or could not have) gotten before. It introduces them to the specifics of a particular business, industry, or professional field and should give them a taste of what working in that field is like. It allows them to practice their communication skills in a substantive manner and serve as a springboard to their future employment. The sponsoring organization should also benefit from the work that the students provide and through the opportunities to maintain ties with the university community, from which many of its future employees may come.

A good internship will provide students with valuable work experiences that help prepare them for full-time employment after graduation. It will also provide several benefits to the school and to the sponsoring organization.

Who Should Intern

IT TAKES A PARTICULAR KIND OF student to succeed in a communication internship. Regardless of the type of job, successful interns always need to have strong communication skills. This includes the ability to write clearly, to speak confidently to clients, coworkers, and superiors, and to use nonverbal behaviors appropriately and effectively. It is also important that interns be self-motivated. Mentors are often extremely busy people who will rely on their interns to learn quickly, take initiative, and sometimes work with little or no direct supervision, so being self-motivated can be especially important. Successful interns are also organized, efficient, and respectful of their mentors and coworkers.

On the other hand, you do not necessarily need to have a clearly defined career path to be a successful intern. Often, students approach the internship as a way to find out whether they enjoy working in a particular field or in a specific position, and the internship can be an excellent way to "test the waters." In fact, some of the most important internship experiences involve learning about career paths you *don't* want to pursue before committing to a certain career. So, don't worry if you're not entirely sure what type of career you'd like to pursue just yet—for your internship, it's much more important that you learn all you're able to learn and do the best work that you can.

Finding an Internship

SOMETIMES THE MOST CHALLENGING part of doing an internship is simply finding one. You may be approaching this task with a number of questions: What type of job do I want? Should I work in a large company or a small business? Who does the type of work I am interested in? Where will I find the right internship for me?

Students generally employ one of two strategies when finding their internships. Some select from among pre-approved opportunities. Several companies and organizations probably contact your school each year to indicate that they are interested in having interns work at their job sites. Once these organizations are approved as sponsors, their internships are advertised to students who are looking. These internships span a full range of opportunities, from working for professional sports teams, radio stations, or airlines to tutoring special needs children or preparing public relations campaigns or working in the governor's office. Some of these internships may be for offices and departments at your college, while most are for organizations in the surrounding community and a few are located out of the state or even out of the country. Some of the internships are paid and several others provide various types of work incentives. Besides the spectrum of opportunities these internships provide, they are also pre-approved by your university, which means less time and paperwork for those students who select from among them.

Many other students find their internships on their own. In some cases, students have not found an opportunity from the pre-approved list that interests them; in other cases, they wish to work at a specific company that has not had interns from the university before. Sometimes the students have talked with their prospective mentors before applying to the internship program, and sometimes the students simply call or visit prospective sponsoring organizations to see if they would be interested in supervising their internship. In any event, students who find their own internships must have their mentors complete paperwork that is submitted to the school. The internship director will then determine whether the mentor and the internship are appropriate.

Choosing the Right Internship for You

IF YOU'RE LIKE MANY STUDENTS, you may have come across more than one internship opportunity that appeals to you. How do you decide which one is best? We recommend that you take several things into consideration. First, think about your interests and what you like to do. Your internship experience will be far more rewarding if you will be spending your time doing work you find interesting and enjoyable. Second, consider what is important to you in a work environment. Are flexible work hours important to you? How about location: How far are you willing or able to commute? Is it is important that you find a paid internship? Are you looking for a formal business environment or someplace with a more casual work atmosphere? Sponsoring organizations will vary considerably on these and other features. Third, think about why you want to do an internship in the first place. Are you looking for an internship that could possibly turn into a permanent job, or are you simply wanting to get experience that will help you find a job elsewhere? Do you have a clearly defined career goal and want to do an internship in that specific field, or are you using the internship to try out working in a certain field, to see if you like it? To find the most fulfilling internship you can, we recommend that you take all of these considerations into account.

Applying for the Internship

SEVERAL SPONSORING ORGANIZATIONS (particularly those we work with on an ongoing basis) have an application and selection process they em-

> *Figure 1.1*
>
> ### Finding an Internship on Your Own
>
> If you decide to find your own internship opportunity, rather than take an internship that has been pre-approved by the school, here are some ideas that can help you find one.
>
> - Think about the industry in which you'd like to work and search for companies in that field. If you want to work in marketing, for instance, make a list of all the marketing firms in your area. You can find lists of these companies in the telephone book, in the placement office or career center at your university, and on the many Web sites that host databases full of internship opportunities (e.g., internship-programs.com or internweb.com). Once you've located prospective companies, call their personnel offices to see if they have any need for interns.
>
> - If it's important to you to work close to home, contact those companies in your area and see if they have any needs for interns (but make sure you know what each company does before you call!). You might also think about doing an internship on campus. Several offices and programs at your university could probably use the help of an intern.
>
> - You might try thinking of people you know and seeing if they have internship opportunities where they work. Sometimes the best opportunities come through personal contact.
>
> - If you're stumped, try looking in the "help wanted" section of the classified ads. This can give you some ideas about what companies are looking for, even though you would be contacting them about an internship rather than a permanent job.

ploy for students wishing to do internships. Some have written application forms that you will need to complete; some will conduct telephone interviews with prospective interns; and some will wish to conduct face-to-face interviews at their job sites. Students must be flexible with these application procedures and treat the interviews as respectfully and seriously as they would any other type of job interview.

If you are asked to take part in a telephone or face-to-face interview, we recommend you use that opportunity to find out as much about the sponsoring organization, and the internship opportunity, as you can. Certainly, the organization will want to find out more about you to determine whether you are a good "fit" for its needs, but an interview can be just as valuable to you as a means of learning whether this is the right internship opportunity for you to pursue. We will discuss the art of job interviewing in detail in Chapter Ten; you might skip ahead and review that material if you are being asked to interview for your internship. However, you should keep a few simple tips in mind that will help you make the most out of an internship interview:

- Get plenty of rest the night before, so you will feel your best during the interview.

- Confirm your interview appointment with a phone call the day before your interview.

- Dress as you would for a regular job interview at that company.

- Bring a copy of your resume with you.

- Be courteous to everyone you interact with. Managers often ask office staff for their impressions of a job candidate.

Figure 1.2

Things to Consider When Deciding on an Internship

Here are a few things to keep in mind when you are choosing an internship.

- How far is it from where I live? Do I have reliable transportation? Is parking available at my job site?

- Is there a specified work schedule or will I be able to fit my work schedule around my classes?

- Will evening or weekend work be involved?

- How clearly has the company defined my responsibilities? How do I feel about those responsibilities? Will they utilize my communication skills?

- Will I be able to fulfill my required number of hours and still meet my other commitments?

- What will I be expected to wear at work? Do I have the appropriate wardrobe?

- Will this internship help me when I am looking for a permanent job?

Negotiating an Internship Offer

LET'S SAY THAT YOU HAVE PASSED the application and interview processes and the sponsoring organization has offered you the internship. Congratulations! Now, how do you come to an agreement on the specifics of your internship assignment that you can both live with?

You should realize, first of all, that some organizations will be more willing than others to negotiate the terms of your internship with you. Keep in mind that, unlike permanent employees, interns are almost always temporary workers, so some sponsors feel less motivated to ne-

gotiate the specifics of their interns' work assignments. However, before agreeing to take on an internship, you must be relatively certain that the work duties, hours, and levels of responsibility will be right for you, and sometimes that requires some tactful negotiation with your potential sponsor.

One tool that will aid you in coming to an agreement with your sponsor is the *internship contract* (located in Appendix A). All students complete this form at the start of their internships, whether they have found the internships on their own

or not. Here, you and your sponsor will clearly define the duties of your internship and the types of work it will involve. You will sign the contract, as will your sponsor, and these signatures indicate your agreement to abide by the specifics of what is described. We will discuss the contract in more detail in Chapter Two.

What Your Internship Should (and Should Not) Involve

BESIDES TAKING INTO ACCOUNT your personal considerations (such as work hours or commuting distance), you will also need to consider the content of the job itself. There are certain types of work experiences that your internship should involve, and certain others that it should not. In general, your internship should prepare you for occupations to which a college graduate with a degree in communication would aspire. That means your internship should involve levels of responsibility and expertise that go beyond the kinds of work that college students typically do. Specifically, most of the work you would be doing should be *substantive* and *communication-oriented*.

Substantive work is the kind of work that makes genuine contributions to the needs and purposes of the organization. In an advertising firm this might include doing market research or assisting with client accounts; in a museum this might include helping to prepare exhibits or giving guided tours. Communication-oriented work is that which makes use of your communication skills. Activities like writing press releases or speaking to groups are exercising your communication abilities; activities like shuttling cars or nailing up signs are not.

Nearly as important as what your internship involves is what is should *not* involve. We fully expect that your internship will involve at least some mundane or menial tasks, such as typing, answering the phone, or cleaning up after events. These types of duties can contribute to the day-to-day operations of your organization and it is not uncommon for them to be assigned to interns. However, we will expect that no more than about 20% of your workload to be of this nature. That is, at least 80% of the work you do as an intern should be substantive and communication-oriented, not clerical or menial. If you find that your supervisors are assigning you a greater share of clerical or menial work, you will need to inform your faculty internship director.

Setting Realistic Expectations

BEFORE BEGINNING ANY INTERNSHIP, we recommend that you and your potential sponsor agree to as detailed a description of your projected duties as possible. This protects both of you and helps everyone to enter the internship experience with clear expectations. Keep in mind, too, that you must enter your internship with expectations that are realistic. While your work should be substantive, it is unlikely that any organization will have you managing accounts or running departments. Just like employees, interns must usually "start at the bottom and work their way up." We say this not to dis-courage you or to keep you from striving to advance, but to prepare you for the reality of working life. Few people, in any type of business or profession, start at the top—and the truth is, they would rarely be effective if they did. Every field is different, and in order to manage operations and people effectively, you must start at the ground level and learn the jobs, the needs, and the specifics of the operations and people you may one day supervise.

Interns and their mentors should be as specific as they can when agreeing on the intern's duties. However, they should also allow the internship to evolve and change as the intern gains experience.

Summary

A NUMBER OF CONSIDERATIONS go into finding and accepting a communication internship. Some have to do with your skills, your interests, and your needs. Others have to do with the organization and what it is looking for. Still others relate to the type of work the internship entails and whether it is appropriate and beneficial. We hope that by taking these issues into account, you will be able to identify an internship opportunity that will be enjoyable, useful, and a memorable part of your undergraduate experience.

Review Questions

1. Why do I want to do an internship? Why now?

2. What kind of work am I most interested in doing as part of my internship?

3. What should my internship involve? What should it not involve?

For Further Reading

Sweitzer, H. F., & King, M. A. (1999). *The successful internship: Transformation and empowerment.* Pacific Grove, CA: Brooks/Cole.

Chapter Two

Understanding Roles, Rules, and Responsibilities

THROUGHOUT YOUR internship, you will be in contact with a number of individuals who will play a role in helping you to succeed. It is important for you to know who these people are and what their individual responsibilities are, so that you will know whom to contact when you need particular forms of assistance. The purpose of this chapter is to detail the roles and responsibilities of all of the key players in your internship experience: your mentor, the personnel at your school, and you. We will also be discussing your internship contract and the many laws and regulations that are applicable to your work as an intern.

Roles and Responsibilities of Your Mentor

THE PERSON MOST IMPORTANT to you at your job site will be your mentor. This will be an employee of your company or organization who will supervise you and evaluate your work. This may be the same person who selected you when you applied for the internship, or it may be the manager or supervisor in whose department you are working. With respect to your internship, your mentor's primary responsibilities are to assign you work, to instruct you as to how and when the work is to be completed, and to evaluate your efforts as an intern. This person will also sign your time log to verify the hours that you work and will communicate with the internship director if any problems arise during your internship.

As with any supervisor, you should communicate often with your mentor about the work you are doing. Chances are good that you will be asked to do things you have never done before, perhaps even things that you don't know how to do. This is part of the great learning experience that internships entail—but you must remember to ask questions and solicit feedback from your mentor to make certain you are learning the tasks properly and performing them adequately. Of course, if not all of your work seems exciting or glamorous, keep in mind that you are there to learn!

At two points during the semester—in the middle of the semester and again at the end—we will ask your mentor to formally evaluate your work. The midterm evaluation is done using a standard evaluation form that is included in Appendix B of this book. We will be asking your mentor to complete this form and then to go over the evaluation with you. You will notice that both you and your mentor are required to sign the form before you turn it in—this is to encourage you and your mentor to communicate with each other about your performance. We recommend that you use this occasion to bring up any questions or issues that are of concern to you in your internship, in the hopes that you might work together to address them during the second half of the semester. In addition to the formal midterm evaluation, you may want to meet with your mentor in the early weeks of your internship (well before your midterm evaluation) to ask for an informal assessment of your strengths and weaknesses thus far. This may help you and your sponsor clear up any misunderstandings about your responsibilities early in your internship.

At the end of the semester we will ask your mentor to evaluate you again, but this time we will ask that the evaluation be written in the form of a letter of recommendation on official letterhead. We suggest that you ask your mentor to print and sign two copies of this evaluation, because you will be handing in one copy in your internship class and you should keep a copy for your own records.

As an intern, you may be asked to perform tasks you have never done before, even tasks you don't know how to do. Keep in mind that this is part of the learning experience!

Roles and Responsibilities of the School

THE INDIVIDUAL AT YOUR school who will be most important to your success as an intern will be the faculty internship director. This is usually (although not always) a full-time faculty member who has direct responsibility over the internship program. If your department has an internship course, this is usually the person who teaches it, develops the syllabus, and assigns your final grade. He or she generally approves companies and organizations as internship sponsors and oversees the types of work those sponsors assign to their student interns.

If you are having difficulties with your mentor or with the work you are being assigned, contact the director. If you wish to do an internship that is not pre-approved or if you have questions about which internships are appropriate, contact the director. If your mentor wishes to speak with someone in the internship program, have him or her contact the director.

The other person at your school with whom you will probably have some contact regarding your internship is your academic advisor. This is sometimes a faculty member and sometimes a staff person who assists students with planning their course schedules and making sure they meet their degree requirements. You are probably already familiar with your academic advisor. This is the person to contact if you have any questions about how many internship credits you need or whether the internship course will contribute to your graduation requirements.

Roles and Responsibilities of the Intern

OF COURSE, WE CANNOT FORGET the very important role that you play in your own internship. No single person will affect the success of your internship experience as much as you will. Your responsibilities actually begin long before you start working at your job site. First, you must ensure that you submit your completed application to the internship program prior to the deadline, and that you have met (or will have met by the time you start your internship) all of the program prerequisites. Once you have learned that your application has been approved, you may begin the process of identifying your internship. In Chapter One we gave you several ideas and things to consider when looking for internship opportunities; now is the time to put those ideas into action and select the internship

that will give you the most beneficial experience you can have.

One of the most important responsibilities you have when selecting your internship is to communicate with your potential sponsor to find out what would be expected of you. Some internships involve duties that are specified beforehand, while others can be tailored to your specific interests and abilities. Some organizations will want you to follow a defined work schedule while others will allow you to set your own hours. Some internships will require you to work evenings or weekends, or to travel occasionally, and others will not. It is up to you to make certain you have a clear understanding of the requirements and expectations of any internship you are considering.

As you consider which internship is the most appropriate for you, be certain that you have a clear understanding of what will be expected of you.

As you are talking with potential internship sponsors, don't be afraid to be candid about what you're looking for, too. If it's very important to you to have particular work experiences or to learn specific skills during your internship, you should make this known beforehand. That will help potential sponsors to determine whether you are an appropriate candidate for the internships they have to offer. Remember that, just like with a regular job, a good internship involves the proper match between person and position. Open communication with potential sponsors will help in determining whether you are right for the internship *and* whether the internship is right for you.

If you decide to do an internship that is not pre-approved, you will be responsible for having your mentor fill out a Sponsor Application and Contract. These forms are available in Appendix C. The application will ask your mentor to describe the company or organization where the internship will occur and the types of duties it will involve. The contract specifies the legal requirements for an internship sponsor. Your mentor must return these forms to the internship director and the director must approve them before you can begin work.

Once your internship begins, you will have several new responsibilities. The most important is to perform your duties to the best of your ability. This means arriving promptly, dressing appropriately, working professionally, and representing yourself—and your school—well. It also means communicating frequently with your mentor about his or her needs, asking questions when you need to, and being a team player and a good citizen of your company or organization. We will cover several of these considerations in greater detail in this book. You may also be required to participate in an internship class. The class is usually designed to acquaint you with many of the issues you might face as an intern and to help you prepare for your eventual job-seeking efforts.

Although most internships last one semester, some interns decide to extend their internships into a sec-ond semester. Others decide to do a second internship after finishing their first. If you are interested in either of these options, be sure to contact the internship director early in the semester and discuss your plans with him or her.

You can see that your responsibilities as an intern are numerous. Many other people, including your mentor, the internship director, and the administrative personnel will do their best to help make your internship a success, but you will ultimately ensure the quality of your experience by knowing what your responsibilities are and fulfilling them in a timely and professional manner.

When you select the internship you wish to do, you will be asked to complete an internship contract in cooperation with your mentor. Below, we address the specifics of this document and some of the things you should be aware of when you complete it.

The Internship Contract

IN YOUR CONTRACT, YOU AND your mentor will be specifying the details of your internship. These include the duties you will be expected to perform and the schedule you will be expected to follow (if any). This contract will be your formal agreement with your mentor and your sponsoring organization concerning the specifics of your internship responsibilities. (The contract is available in Appendix A.)

When completing your contract, we recommend that you encourage your mentor to be as detailed as possible with respect to the description of your duties. Instead of writing "administrative duties," for instance, ask your mentor to specify the exact responsibilities you will be expected to perform. Of course, mentors will vary in terms of the level of detail they can provide; if they regularly have interns, they may be able to be more spe-cific as to the job duties than if they have never supervised interns before. The more detailed your contract, however, the more you and your mentor will know what to expect of each other.

As you and your mentor are discussing your responsibilities, keep two things in mind. First, the internship program requires that no more than 20% of your work be clerical or menial in nature: things like answering telephones, typing, filing, working a cash register, tending bar, stuffing envelopes, or handing out samples. Many internships will involve at least a little of this type of work, but the vast majority of your work must be substantive; that is, it must deal with the substance of the profession in which you're working and be the kind of experience that can help you in your career goals. If it appears that too much of your work will be menial, the internship director will not approve your contract, even if both you and your mentor have agreed to it.

Second, it is often the case that internship responsibilities will change over time. Perhaps you are a quick learner and your mentor decides that you should be given more complex responsibilities than were originally suggested. The school expects a certain amount of change and development in most internships. However, if your mentor makes changes in your job responsibilities that you are uncomfortable with, we recommend that you let the internship director know. He or she will advise you as to your options and may decide to speak with your mentor about the situation.

You will notice that both you and your mentor must sign and date your contract. This solidifies your agreement with each other and signals your intention to take the agreement seriously. Your contract will be due during the first week of the semester in which you are doing your internship. If you extend your internship into a second semester you may not need to sign a new contract, but if you do a second internship, or if you change internships during the semester, you will need to write and sign a new contract.

Laws and Regulations Applicable to Your Internship

NO TEXTBOOK CAN, OR SHOULD, purport to advise you on the complex legal issues that surround employment in today's workforce. However, we can introduce you to some of the concerns that may have an effect on your career. To begin with, there is a possibility that your status as an intern will raise questions or issues not present in other employment situations. We will briefly address these issues before turning to more general matters.

The question of whether or not you are paid for your work as an intern is a matter that you negotiate with your sponsoring organization. If you are not being paid, then federal law requires that your internship meet three criteria: 1) it must be part of a structured educational program; 2) your sponsoring organization must not receive substantial benefit from your work; and, 3) there can be no promise of a job after completion of the internship. The first requirement is met by your participation in this internship class. The second criterion is met in any internship in which you are learning a substantial amount from your work experiences; in this way, your sponsoring organization is providing you with an educational benefit that offsets any benefits it receives from your work. Finally, there is nothing to prevent you from seeking and obtaining a permanent job with your sponsoring organization. But, there can be no *promise* of such a job at the start of your internship (Gross, 1993, p. 11).

If you are paid for your internship, federal law requires that you make at least minimum wage. You may be reimbursed for expenses, but this should be done as an actual reimbursement for amounts spent (usually you will be required to submit receipts before receiving reimbursements) (Gross, 1993, pp. 11-12). We raise these issues here primarily to inform you of what you can expect from an employer, but your status as paid or unpaid may also be relevant in the event you are injured while working at your internship.

If you are being paid for your work, then Worker's Compensation statutes will apply to your internship. If you are unpaid, you will not be covered by Worker's Compensation, but you *may* be covered under your sponsoring organization's liability insurance. This is a question you will want to raise with your mentor/supervisor when you discuss the terms of your internship.

Pay or other benefits of your internship must be negotiated with the sponsoring organization at the time you begin work.

Employment Discrimination and Harassment

ONE OF THE MORE IMPORTANT WAYS in which the law can affect your employment is through federal and state regulation of workplace discrimination and harassment. Federal law prohibits employment discrimination on the basis of race, sex, national origin, religion, age, or marital status (42 USCS § 2000 et seq.). In addition, the Americans with Disabilities Act prohibits discrimination on the basis of disability status and also requires that reasonable accommodations be made in order to permit qualified persons to accept and continue employment in many circumstances (42 USCS § 12101 et seq.). State law concerning these issues may vary to some degree, but most will closely parallel the federal law. For this reason, we will discuss the federal statutes and standards in this chapter.

Employment discrimination is most readily thought of as treating a person differently from similarly situated persons on the basis of one or more characteristics, such as race or gender. One particular form of discrimination is sexual harassment. Sexual harassment protects people from unwanted conduct of a sexual nature on the job in certain circumstances. Sexual harassment can take one of two forms. The first is called *quid pro quo* harassment, which literally means "this for that." In this form of harassment a benefit is promised in exchange for sexual favors (e.g., "If you sleep with me, I'll promote you to manager") or a detriment is threatened if the receiving party does not comply (e.g., "Go out with me, or I'll give you a poor performance review"). Although such a direct ultimatum is easy to identify as *quid pro quo* harassment, the harassment does not have to be made explicit. A supervisor is prohibited from giving a poor performance review to an employee just because he refused her advances, even if she never explicitly threatened to do so. The second form of harassment is called "hostile work environment," and it involves conduct of a sexual nature that "has the purpose or effect of unreasonably interfering with an individual's work performance or creating an intimidating, hostile, or offensive working environment" (Federal Register 45, November 10, 1980, pp. 74675-74677). Whether or not conduct rises to the level of harassment is measured with reference to a "reasonable person standard." This means that it is not the intent of the person engaging in the conduct that matters; the relevant question is whether a reasonable person would find the conduct offensive (Federal Register 45, November 10, 1980, pp. 74675-74677).

This discussion is not intended to put you in a state of hypersensitivity. Instead, it is intended to alert you to an issue that may arise in your workplace and that has a strong communication component to it. As a communication student, you have likely had some exposure to discussions of how men and women communicate differently. Similarly, you have probably been asked to consider differences in communication behaviors related to cultural differences. In our most basic discussions of communication as a process, we begin with the idea that each person has a particular frame of reference that serves as his or her window into the world. Given that we, as communication students, understand a great deal about how and why people interpret messages differently, we are in strong positions to understand how workplace interactions can be most effectively handled. You may not be able to avoid harassment altogether, but you may be able to prevent errors in judgment from escalating into serious problems.

Summary

IN THIS CHAPTER WE HAVE DISCUSSED the roles and responsibilities of the various people who will help to make your internship a success. You should feel free to contact these people as different needs arise. We have also given you an introduction to some of the rules and regulations that can affect your work as an intern. In the next chapter, we will offer some general advice about what to expect during your first days on the job, and some of the issues that you need to be aware of as you begin your work as an intern.

Review Questions

1. What do I perceive are the responsibilities of my internship?

2. What should be specified in my internship contract?

3. Why do you think the authors chose to discuss discrimination and harassment in a book about internships? Why would interns in particular need to know about this topic? Are interns more or less likely to be on the giving or receiving end of sexual harassment?

For Further Reading

Clair, R. P. (1993). The use of framing devices to sequester organizational narratives: Hegemony and harassment. *Communication Monographs, 60,* 113-136.

Clair, R. P., Chapman, P. A., & Kunkel, A. W. (1996). Narrative approaches to raising consciousness about sexual harassment: From research to pedagogy and back again. *Journal of Applied Communication Research, 24,* 241-259.

Quinn, B. A. (2000). The paradox of complaining: Law, humor, and harassment in the everyday work world. *Law and Social Inquiry, 25,* 1151-1185.

Chapter Three

Your First Days on the Job

REGARDLESS OF WHETHER you have held several jobs in your lifetime or your internship is your first real work experience, the beginning days on the job can be a little overwhelming. You may wonder whether or not you'll fit in with the other employees. Maybe you'll feel as though there is more to know than you'll ever be able to learn. Perhaps the work environment seems strange to you, or you feel a bit lost because you're not sure what to do or how to do it. If you experience any of this, relax; these thoughts and feelings are completely normal. They come from our natural discomfort with uncertainty. Whenever people are put into situations in which they don't know what to expect, their levels of uncertainty about those situations rise, and so, too, do their levels of frustration, nervousness, and discomfort (see, e.g., Berger & Calabrese, 1975).

Our goal in this chapter is to help you to reduce some of that uncertainty by walking you through some of the major issues you'll face during your first days on the job. We will discuss meeting your coworkers and your mentor (if you haven't already), figuring out the culture and expectations of your organization, learning your responsibilities, and completing some of the paperwork that will be required of you at this point in your internship. We will also address ways to manage your image and your relationships with the others in your organization. Again, we want to stress that every intern—and every internship—is different, and some of the issues we discuss will apply to certain internship situations more than to others.

Many people feel nervous and uncertain when they start a new job or internship. These feelings are completely natural, but they do motivate us to learn and explore.

Meeting Your Mentor and Coworkers

ONE OF THE BIGGEST CHALLENGES many people face when they begin a new job is meeting their coworkers...and remembering their names! If you think back to your first days of college, you'll probably remember what it was like to be in large classes with students and professors you didn't know. Maybe you lived in a residence hall, sorority, or fraternity, and can remember how long it took you to get to know the other residents. Starting work at an unfamiliar organization is much the same. One thing to keep in mind is that getting to know people will take some time, particularly if your organization is large. So, try not to feel overwhelmed if you have trouble remembering people's names during your first days on the job. When it takes us a long time to get to know people, they often end up becoming some of our closest friends!

Some interns will meet their mentors before starting work, and others will not. If you work in a large organization, your mentor may not be the same person who selected you to be an intern. In this case, you will probably be meeting your mentor for the first time at the start of your job. In other cases, you may have interviewed, or at least spoken with, your mentor before reporting for work. Whatever the situation, you will probably meet with your mentor several times over the first couple of weeks at your internship. As we discussed in Chapter Two, your mentor's primary responsibility is to assign you your duties and teach you how to fulfill them.

As you interact with your mentor during your first days on the job, the nature of your internship responsibilities should be made clear to you. This process is generally a positive one because it reduces your level of uncertainty and should make you feel more at ease with your mentor, the organization, and your internship. Sometimes, however, interns feel a little disillusioned if they learn that their responsibilities aren't what they had in mind when they signed on. Perhaps you're working in an advertising firm, and instead of writing press releases or designing television commercials, your mentor has you proofreading advertising copy or "shadowing" an account manager. Maybe you feel like this is a waste of your time, or that these are not the types of duties you expected to be doing.

Bear in mind that mentors will often have their interns start slowly by giving them low-level responsibilities or by asking them to observe how other people work. This is to be expected; recall from our discussion in Chapter One that your internship is a chance to *learn* and that you will probably not be managing accounts or supervising major projects right away. If your mentor starts you off with lower-level responsibilities than you expected, he or she is probably trying to accomplish two things. The first is to help you learn the nuts and bolts of whatever profession or industry you're working in. Work is like school, athletics, or the military: you begin at the bottom and work your way up. This isn't to punish you or hold you back—it's to make sure that, when you do advance, you advance with the knowledge, skills, and experience that will make

you effective at what you're doing. Imagine the young man or woman who, never having played basketball before, is immediately made a starter on the varsity team. Without having mastered the fundamentals of dribbling, passing, shooting, guarding, and blocking, this young player could not possibly be effective and would probably end up costing the team many victories.

Accepting that you must begin with the fundamentals and work your way up is one sign of a mature and responsible worker, so the second thing your mentor is trying to accomplish by giving you low-level responsibilities is to see if you have that maturity. Particularly if you are very excited about your job, you may be anxious to do the "real work" and may feel like you are being held back by having to do the basics. But, if you can keep in mind that mastering the basics will help you be effective at higher-level responsibilities, that will help you realize that your mentor is

really doing you a huge favor—and your mentor will notice your positive attitude. Your mentor will be looking to see that you understand the value of learning and mastering the basics, and if you do, he or she will have greater confidence in your ability to handle more complex—and more exciting—responsibilities.

One word of caution about your duties, though. Although a mature intern accepts that he or she must "start at the bottom" in an organization, that does not mean that your mentor should be assigning you duties that are substantially different than the ones you agreed to. As we have discussed in the previous two chapters, if you find that your workload is nothing but clerical work or menial labor, or if the work you're doing is considerably different than what was described in your contract, you need to contact the internship director and explain the situation.

Making a Good First Impression

AS THE OLD ADAGE GOES, YOU never have a second chance to make a good first impression. This is more true than you probably realize. According to a principle known as the *primacy effect*, the first impression you make on people is more powerful than your second, or third, or any other impression when it comes to forming an overall image of you. Of course, we all know that first impressions are sometimes very misleading—you can probably think of at least one friend who you never thought you'd become friends with when you first met him or her. Yes,

our impressions of people *can* change over time, but the first impression is still critical. After all, you still *remember* your first impression of that friend you didn't think you'd like, don't you?

The good news about the primacy effect is that if you make a positive first impression on people, they will be prone to like and respect you even if you make mistakes later. That is, a good first impression will make up for more negative impressions you might make later on. Of course, the bad news is that if you

make a bad first impression, it will be all that much harder for you to correct it later. Can you see how important your first impression is?

So, how do you make it a positive one? The first answer that many

---

Accepting that you must begin with the fundamentals and work your way up is one sign of a mature and responsible intern.

---

people think of is by looking nice. Your appearance will be especially important during your first days on the job, as people are forming their initial impressions of you. When it comes to judging other people, human beings instinctively give a great deal of weight to visual cues, such as those produced by clothing, grooming, and accessories. In our ancestry, this was largely for protection—in order to survive, early humans needed to be able to tell friends from foes quickly, with a simple glance. That instinct is still with us today, although it is now more refined: modern humans use visual cues to make judgments about others' credibility, intelligence,

competence, friendliness, and many other qualities. Often, a person's appearance can lead others to make judgments about him or her that are simply not accurate— but those judgments will lead to impressions that will be difficult to change later on. So, unless our appearance helps us make a positive first impression on others, we may never get the chance to make a second impression. We will discuss personal appearance in more detail in Chapter Five.

As you know, though, your image is not entirely about your physical appearance. Many other things will influence the impressions peo-

ple form of you, including your attitudes, your behavior toward others, and how well you do your job. Whenever you begin a new position, it is worth taking some time to think specifically about the kind of impression you would like others to have of you. Do you want to be seen as professional? Easygoing? Mature? Friendly and outgoing? Responsible? No matter what you want your image to be, it will be due in large part to the way you act toward others on the job, particularly during the first days of your assignment.

Understanding the Culture of Your Organization

YOU MAY BE ABLE TO REMEMBER the first time you met someone with a different cultural background than yours. Perhaps you met this person through a club, or he or she was an exchange student at your school. Whatever the situation, you probably realized that some of this person's experiences, ideas, and values were different than yours. Interacting with people from other cultures fascinates—and frustrates— us because we lack a common experience. But what is culture, exactly, and why do people from different cultures have such a hard time understanding each other?

A large part of the answer is that a culture represents a shared set of values, beliefs, customs, and expectations. In some cultures, for instance, it is traditional for men to be breadwinners and women to keep house; in other cultures, this is not necessarily the norm. Some cultures are individualistic, in that

A good first impression pays off in a number of ways. By contrast, it is difficult to recover from a bad first impression. Consider the impression you want to make.

they value individual achievement and "being all you can be." Other cultures are collectivistic; they value foresaking individual achievement for the good of the group. It is easy to see how people raised with such different ways of thinking can experience conflict and misunderstanding when they try to communicate.

As you begin your internship, it will be important for you to realize that every organization has its own culture—its own customs, expectations, and values—and you should make it your business to learn what that culture is. Some companies have a culture of formality, in which people are addressed by their titles, personal appearance is

expected to be conservative, and an air of decorum is maintained. Other companies, of course, have a culture of informality, in which more casual dress and behavior are the norm. Many companies have particular traditions or specific values that can be traced back to their founders. Whatever the situation, it serves you well to learn all you can about your organization's culture so that you will know what is appropriate to wear, to talk about, to call people, and to do while on the job. Knowing the cultural expectations that define your organization will help keep you from committing the types of mistakes that others will experience as "culture shock."

Learning Your Job Responsibilities

EVERY INTERN LEARNS HIS OR HER job responsibilities a little differently. In some cases, your duties may be predefined and explicit. If you are working in an organization that has interns regularly, your mentor may be able to give you a very specific set of job responsibilities. In other cases, though, mentors may formulate your responsibilities as you progress through your internship, changing your responsibilities as they have the opportunity to observe how you perform. In still other cases, you may find that you are given little guidance about what you should be doing.

Whatever the situation, keep in mind that learning your job responsibilities is a process that will likely last well into your internship semester. Unless you have a predefined and repetitive set of duties, your job

description may very well change and develop over the course of your semester. Sometimes it may feel as though you have just mastered your duties when they are suddenly being changed, but remember that a good internship will expose you to many different sides of your industry or profession, so breadth in your duties is often a good thing.

How will you learn about your responsibilities? It may be from your mentor. He or she should certainly give you work assignments and teach you the skills you need to accomplish them. It may be from working with other interns. If there are several interns in your organization, they can often be a valuable source of information about how to excel at your job. And it may be from other employees be-

sides your mentor who can help you to "learn the ropes." In truth, you will probably learn a little bit about your responsibilities from many different people—not just what your responsibilities *are*, but how to accomplish them effectively. Your ability to keep your eyes and ears open and to learn from others will be a great benefit to you as an intern. While your mentor and other employees will tell you how to complete various tasks, you will also need to actively participate in this learning process by seeking information on your own. Figure 3.1 lists several information seeking tactics that newcomers to organizations use as they attempt to learn about their jobs.

Your Paperwork

DURING THE INITIAL DAYS OF YOUR internship, you will be responsible for completing at least two pieces of paperwork that must be turned in to the internship director: the internship contract and your time log. Here, we will briefly describe each of these; actual due dates for their completion will be provided to you by the internship director.

We discussed your *internship contract* in detail in Chapter Two. This form describes the nature of your responsibilities as an intern, and it is signed by you and your mentor. It is generally due by the end of the first week of the semester. Many students will turn in this form before

their internships begin, but others will hold onto the form in order to complete it during the first few days on the job. In either event, be certain that it is completely filled out and that both you and your mentor have signed and dated it. Remember, this is a formal agreement between you and your mentor, so it should be completed with care and turned in to the internship director by the prescribed due date.

You will need to complete part of your *time log* at the start of your internship, and then again every week. This form will be the official record of your hours worked. At

the end of every week, you will write in the number of hours you worked during that one-week period and the total number of hours you have accumulated up to that point. You must then have your mentor sign and date the form on the line next to these figures. At the end of the semester, after your mentor has verified your total number of hours worked, you will turn in the time log to the internship director. You will find your time log in Appendix D.

An important word of advice about all of your paperwork: it is your responsibility to make sure that every required form is completed, signed, and turned in by the appropriate due date. This will require you to plan ahead—if, for instance, your mentor is going to be out of town when a particular form is due, it is your responsibility to get his or her signature ahead of time, or else to ask another supervisor to sign it in your mentor's place. You need to be aware that the due dates will be enforced, and if your mentor cannot or does not sign your forms in time, it will be *you* who suffers the consequence of a reduced grade. So, plan ahead!

Figure 3.1

Newcomer Information-Seeking Tactics: How New Employees Learn about Their Jobs

Overt questions: You seek information by asking someone an open and direct question. Example: "How much time are we given for lunch?"

Indirect questions: You try to learn something by asking about it in a less direct, non-interrogative way or by hinting. Example: "Do many people leave the office for lunch?"

Third-party questions: Rather than asking the person directly, you ask someone else who would know. Example: "Do you think Pam would mind if we took a full hour for lunch?"

Disguising conversations: You try to learn something by disguising an information-seeking attempt as though it were a natural part of the discussion. Example: "I guess Pam won't mind if we take a full hour for lunch."

Testing limits: You seek information by doing something questionable and seeing how others respond. This is a very risky way to seek information and can cause you to make a poor impression. Example: Rather than asking anyone, you take full hour for lunch and watch how others react when you return.

Observing: You learn by simply watching what others do in relevant situations. Example: Rather than asking anyone, you watch how long others take for their lunch break.

Surveillance: You solicit information by reflecting on past behaviors you've observed. Example: You wonder about how long a lunch break you can take, and you remember that two people in your department have taken a full hour twice this week and no one has seemed to notice or care.

Adapted from: Miller, V. D., & Jablin, F. M. (1991). Information seeking during organizational entry: Influences, tactics, and a model of the process. *Academy of Management Review, 16*, 92-120.

Learning to Work with Staff

A FINAL NOTE ABOUT YOUR FIRST days on the job concerns your ability to work well with the other employees and staff members at your organization. We hope that your interactions with these people will be positive, and that the employees will welcome you and offer their assistance. If you find that this is not the case, there may be several reasons why. One is simply that the employees, like you, are busy people who may not have a great deal of extra time to offer. They may be reluctant to take the time to get to know you because they have seen so many interns come and go over the years. Particularly if you are working in a high-stress environment, such as in an advertising agency or a television studio, you may feel that other employees are disregarding you and what you have to offer. If you find yourself in this type of situation, try not to be offended by it. Keep in mind that the employees are working against deadlines and may be under a great deal of stress to produce—and we all know how impatient we can get with others when we're under stress.

Although it happens infrequently, it may also be the case that you perceive feelings of jealousy toward you on the part of other employees. Let's say that your mentor, because he or she wants you to learn, gives you special assignments that are not generally made available to some of the lower-level employees.

It would be easy to see how some of those employees may feel slighted and may be jealous of you and the special treatment you are receiving. In other instances, employees may be jealous of the attention you're getting as the new person in the organization. If you perceive these types of feelings being directed at you, keep two things in mind. First, jealousy is a

natural human emotion that we all experience from time to time, and it will eventually fade. Second, the employees in these scenarios don't resent you personally; they are simply jealous because you are being treated differently than they are. That is, they would feel jealous no matter who the intern was.

Figure 3.2

Important Paperwork at the Start of Your Internship

Internship Contract: Must be completed and signed by you and your mentor. Due the first week of your internship.

Sponsor Application and Contract: Must be completed by your mentor if you are not doing a pre-approved internship. Due the first week of your internship.

Time Log: Completed by you and signed by your mentor every week. You will bring the time log cover sheet to class to be checked at specified times throughout the semester, and you will turn it in during the last week of the semester.

Note: Your internship director may require additional paperwork that is not listed here.

Summary

YOUR FIRST DAYS ON THE JOB WILL be memorable, and in many ways they will set the tone for the rest of your internship experience. Of course, one of the most important aspects of that experience will be the working relationship you have with your mentor, and it is toward this topic that we turn our attention in the next chapter.

Review Questions

1. How can I make a good first impression on my mentor and coworkers?

2. Mistakes, wrong impressions, and embarrassing situations are common during the early days of a new job, and internships are no different. Discuss one of these you experienced in your internship. With the benefit of hindsight, what have you learned about how to prevent similar negative situations in the future? What do you now wish you'd done differently?

For Further Reading

Albrecht, T. L., & Bach, B. W. (1997). *Communication in complex organizations: A relational approach.* Fort Worth, TX: Harcourt Brace.

Carnegie, D. (1981). *How to win friends and influence people.* New York: Pocket Books.

Chapter Four

Working with Your Mentor

WORKING UNDER THE supervision of another person can be a wonderfully fulfilling and interesting experience. It can also be a real nightmare. Whether you have a good experience or a terrible one may depend a great deal on how well you adjust to working with the particular person you are dealing with. We all have our preferred working styles and personality traits. Some people are better suited to work together than others. In any situation, the working relationship can benefit from skilled communication on the part of one or both of the parties. In this chapter we will walk through a few topics that may help you deal with the practicalities of working with a supervisor and/or mentor.

Common Styles of Mentoring

MANAGEMENT THEORY TELLS US that there are four primary manager/employee types that emerge in the workplace. These are the *hidden, open, closed,* and *blind* types (Hamilton & Parker, 1997). Each type has key characteristics that help predict how such a person will react to conflict, stress, and uncertainty. While people rarely fit within a particular type exactly, most people will show strong tendencies toward one or two types. Knowing what type of manager and/or employee you are can shed some light on what you will be like in relationships with other people. Being aware of your type and the potential problems and benefits associated with that type can help you ward off communication problems and maximize your strong suits.

Beyond the four personality types discussed here, you can classify mentors along a variety of different lines. There are "hands-on" mentors who will want to work closely with you, spend time with you, review your work, and provide extensive feedback. Some mentors are focused on the bottom line and will help you figure out how to get that next promotion or the next big project; they may be particularly savvy at office politics and self-promotion. Other mentors will seem more like a personal friend and will take an interest in the quality of your life and your happiness, along with your success on the job. These mentors may be less apt to involve themselves in your day-to-day career development; they may wait for you to ask them specifically about business or career matters. Of course, some mentors take both career and personal satisfaction very seriously and will be valuable sources of information and advice about achieving both. You may have more than one mentor at a time. You may choose one mentor to help you drive your career in the short term, another to help you stay sane, and a third to help you improve your long-term career trajectory.

Choosing a Mentor

WHEN YOU ARE SEEKING A mentor outside of a formalized supervisor/subordinate relationship, you can use your knowledge of personality types and broad approaches to mentoring to consider whether a potential mentor is a good fit for you. In addition to considering whether your potential mentor has a personal style that coordinates well with your own, you will want to think about other things as well. Perhaps most important, you should ask yourself what you are looking for from a mentoring relationship. Do you want advice? Support? Inside information about your organization? Or, are you looking for an all-around role model? Once you know what you personally want out of the relationship you can decide with whom to cultivate

As you grow professionally, you can become an ally for your mentor, just as he or she is an ally for you.

Figure 4.1

Common Communication Styles

Hamilton and Parker (1997) identified four communication styles and vary along two continua: the use of disclosure and the use of feedback. Disclosure is the "voluntary sharing of information, opinions, and feelings," and feedback is "responses from others in the form of facts, opinions, and feelings" (p. 77). Below are brief descriptions of the four styles and where each falls along these continua.

Closed Style: Low disclosure/low feedback	**Blind Style: High disclosure/low feedback**
Typically, closed style communicators seek little feedback and use very little disclosure. Safety is a primary goal of closed style communicators. They may have trouble expressing their expectations to other people and may not be good at providing constructive criticism. Closed style communicators may ignore conflict and may avoid having to make decisions (unless they can safely rely on policy and procedure to back them up). Closed style communicators are likely to work best on their own, with little interaction or cooperation with other people. They are typically seen as reliable, detail-oriented when it comes to administrative matters, and even-handed when it comes to handling employee matters (such as raises).	Blind style communicators readily share their opinions, ideas, and expertise. On the flipside, they do not actively seek feedback and may not make good use of the feedback they do receive. Blind style communicators are typically good in a crisis situation, when they will often be willing to step in and take charge. However, they have a tendency to see things only in one way (their way). Blind communicators may over-use disclosure by offering opinions, criticisms, or advice where they are not wanted; they may be unable or unwilling to delegate effectively and may become impatient with people who do not conform to their exacting standards.
Hidden Style: Low disclosure/high feedback	**Open Style: High disclosure/high feedback**
The hidden style communicator operates from a strong need for social acceptance. Hidden style communicators use low disclosure tactics, while seeking a great deal of feedback from those around them. The hidden communicator hides his opinions, ideas, and feelings from other people in order to maintain high levels of social acceptance. A hidden communicator is one that will listen as you tell them your thoughts, problems, and life-story, but will not easily reciprocate the disclosure. Hidden communicators can be fun to work with, good at maintaining a pleasant and supportive social environment within an organization, and make sympathetic listeners for people with issues to discuss. However, hidden communicators are more likely to participate in the phenomenon of groupthink.	Open style communicators have a very forward and direct approach to communication that can make other people uncomfortable in its extreme form. Typically, open style communicators seek participation from co-workers and subordinates and encourage two-way communication. In addition to sincerely valuing the participation of other people, the open communicator may readily offer criticism, advice, or expertise to the people around her. This direct approach to disclosure can be disruptive if it comes too fast, too soon, or at inappropriate times. The challenge for open communicators is identifying the right time and method of making disclosures and seeking feedback. Fortunately, open style communicators have room to be flexible in their communication styles *if* they realize that they need to back off of either their disclosure or feedback levels.

relationships. This may sound calculating and to some extent it is. Some mentoring relationships may arise naturally. However, you may find that you want to intentionally cultivate ties with people you don't have an obvious connection with in order to obtain specialized advice or assistance. In these more intentional relationships, both you and your potential mentor must do a type of cost/benefit analysis. As you cultivate a relationship with a mentor, you should be aware of what you have to offer him or her. While you may be in a subordinate position to your mentor, you will still have ideas, expertise, connections, and advice to offer her. As you grow professionally you can become an ally for your mentor and provide increased assistance to him. This network of mutual assistance can be very helpful, both professionally and personally—but it requires extensive time commitments from both you and your mentor; this is why you should not be afraid to bring an evaluative eye to bear on the type and quality of relationships you are developing.

All of this requires that you actively participate in the development of this mentoring relationship. You need not be a wallflower who only speaks when spoken to. Indeed, as you get to know your mentor, it's entirely appropriate and desirable to discuss topics and issues that transcend the tasks at hand, such as career choices, the job market, and key skills your mentor has found useful in their particular line of work. Mentors often enjoy talking about past experiences—successes and mistakes—but they may only do this if you ask. Your best source of "real world" advice could be standing right in front of you, but such a relationship may be difficult to foster if you don't make an effort to get to know your mentor by asking about her opinions and experiences. You may be surprised to find that many people really enjoy talking about themselves!

In the early stages of a developing mentorship relationship, there are a few basic considerations you should keep in mind. You should consider the amount of time the potential mentor will have to devote to you and how much time you might legitimately expect her to devote. How closely aligned are your interests (both personal and professional) with those of your mentor? Will you make a good professional fit, work on similar projects, share common knowledge bases, and have common professional associations? If not, what will hold the relationship together? Answers to this last question will vary: It may be something as broad as personal liking and a supportive friendship or it may be something as narrow as access to a specific body of knowledge or technical expertise. You may want to compare the trajectory of your projected career paths and consider whether the two of you are so close in age or status that you might soon be competing for promotions or clients. If so, ask yourself how you will handle the competition and what the potential costs might be of competing against someone you have a relationship with. Look at the people your potential mentor has relationships with. Are they people you want to work with, learn from, and be associated with by reputation? Also, try to determine whether your potential mentor has healthy relationships with these people, as this may give you some insight into what he or she is really like as a mentor.

If you are working with an assigned supervisor, you may or may not find that this person is also useful as a mentor. To the extent that you can work well with your supervisor you might expect to benefit from that relationship even if it never develops into a true mentorship relationship. Because of the similarity in the two relationships, the keys to making the most of your relationship with a supervisor will be the same as those that are central to working with a self-selected mentor.

Understanding Your Mentor's Expectations

WHETHER YOU ARE WORKING under someone who is actively cultivating you as a protégé or someone who simply needs you to work accurately and efficiently, understanding her expectations for you is critical to having a successful relationship.

The advice we have to give you on this point is somewhat obvious in nature, but often difficult in application. To maximize your ability to meet the expectations of your supervisor/mentor, you need to pull out the stops and maximize your use of effective communication strategies! While presuming that this advice comes as no surprise to you, we also expect that a few more specific ideas might be helpful.

First, foster an open and professional relationship with your mentor. By being upfront about what you expect and what you understand to be her expectations, you can encourage a similar directness in your mentor. Once you create an expectation of honesty and directness, you have to be prepared to deal with negative communication in a professional manner. It is far easier to be open to feedback when the feedback is consistently positive; but when you are faced with criticism or disappointment, it is even more important that you deal with the information in a professional and cooperative manner. Having an open communication system between you and your mentor requires a high level of maturity and professionalism on the side of both parties. This can take time to develop, and every relationship will have different levels of openness. So, to start the ball rolling you should communicate as directly as possible about the issue of *communication*.

Second, ask questions and seek clarification about individual tasks and assignments. This can be a double-edged sword—you want the necessary information but you don't want to appear overly insecure or incapable of executing independent judgments. To strike a useful balance, find simple, precise ways of finding the important information you need for each assignment (or type of assignment). What is the due date or timeline for completion? Should you provide a draft or proposal in advance of the final due date for feedback or approval? What is the ultimate objective of the assignment? Is there an expectation of how much work, time, or other resources that ought to be committed to this assignment?

Who will the final consumers of the project be: clients, the CEO, the media?

When you are new to an organization there will be many questions like these that come up as you learn new tasks. Over time you may find that tasks repeat themselves and you know the answers to most of these questions. In these cases, you may find it useful to ask the question: "Is there anything different about this project that I need to know, or will it follow the same expectations that we've had for prior projects?"

Many times you will be given your instructions orally and you may seek clarification orally. Our advice here is to take notes and keep them until the project is complete. If you find that you are getting confusing or contradicting information from your mentor/supervisor or from several sources at once, this is a time to seek clarification. In these situations it may be useful to reduce your final understanding of the project or assignment to writing, either in a memo or in an e-mail form. Putting things in writing can help you identify areas where you are uncertain or confused and can help your supervisor focus on the content of the messages you are receiving. Some organiza-

tional cultures never use memos, so you may want to go with a less formal e-mail. Or you may want to produce a draft or mock-up and seek feedback in advance of the deadline in order to flush out areas of confusion.

Some supervisors respond very well to requests for clarification and feedback on early stages of project completion. Others do not have the time or the inclination to provide informative communication along the way. In these instances you may find yourself frustrated when you are criticized

Working under the supervision of another person can be a wonderfully fulfilling and interesting experience. It can also be a real nightmare. Whether you have a good experience or a terrible one may depend a great deal on how well you adjust to working with the particular person you are dealing with.

for not giving them what they wanted. This is a difficult situation to address, and you will have to find a method of dealing with it that fits your personality type and your organization's overall culture. Two potential solutions are provided here. First, you can use e-mail messages asking for feedback and clearly stating what assumptions or decisions you are going to make if you do not receive that feedback. Sometimes this will nudge your supervisor into providing you with the necessary information. Second, you can find out at the beginning of the project if there are other people working on it or who have information concerning it. At this time, clearly express your intent to follow up with these people and seek their input if questions arise. In this case, you will want to seek these potential contacts immediately and pave the way for your future questions by politely asking them, in advance, for their assistance. Of course, if you have been fortunate enough to develop a mentoring relationship with someone who has relevant knowledge or expertise, you can always turn to your mentor for informal assistance and feedback.

Having More Than One Supervisor

IF YOU RECEIVE ASSIGNMENTS from, or otherwise report to, more than one supervisor, then you may face problems with time management and prioritizing work assignments. In these instances you must begin by having a realistic expectation for what you can and cannot accomplish at any given time. By identifying your limits—and we all have them—you can avoid some time management problems. As an intern, you may feel particularly uncomfortable telling a supervisor that you can't do something, especially if the person asking for help is someone you haven't already done much work for. One way to handle this awkwardness is to ask your supervisor to help you prioritize your overall workload and to help you evaluate how much time you should commit to each project. In the course of this conversation, you can show your supervisor how much work you have and how long things are taking you to complete. This can be a subtle way of introducing a conversation about your time and resource limitations. Remember, when you have more than one person giving you work, you cannot assume that they all know what you really have going on. By involving one (or more of them) in a prioritizing session, you can provide them with valuable information.

If someone insists that you help him or her with a project that you do not have time to complete, you should probably consult one of your other supervisors. What you do not want to do is leave one person hanging without warning him or her that the problem has arisen. It is not necessarily your place, especially as an intern, to prioritize your own workload. Let the supervisors make the decision on how your time is best spent. As awkward as this may seem, it will be better than disappointing someone unnecessarily. The best way to minimize the awkwardness is to handle the situation in a professional manner and with a problem-solving attitude; approach your supervisor(s) with the question of how best to accomplish your tasks and do the best you can do for all parties involved. Don't panic. Don't become defensive. Don't try to make the situation be about whom is to blame. Be as flexible as you can with your time and, *if possible*, offer to commit additional resources to work during the critical period of time. However, we want to reiterate our initial advice: don't take on more than you can finish in an effort to be a hero.

If you find that you are having repeated problems with too much work or too many competing deadlines crossing your desk, then you may want to set up a fairly formal reporting system—such as a weekly memo or e-mail—that apprises the people you work with of your current projects, whom they are for, their deadlines, and your work schedule (such as days when you will be out of the office for meetings or personal appointments). This will help you keep everyone informed about what you have going on and will give you some documentation to fall back on should someone insist that you help out when you cannot. Even if your supervisors never read these memos from you, you can keep them in a file along with your time logs, appointment calendars, or other project planning devices. As paranoid as it may seem, it is never too early to start considering how you can best present yourself and how you can best document your efforts to work efficiently and effectively. This is especially true in an organization in which internal communication tends not to be strong and people frequently have conflicts over job responsibilities, deadlines, priorities, and resource commitments.

Having more than one supervisor can be complicated. In this situation, it is even more critical that you manage your time appropriately and communicate regularly with your mentors.

Resolving Conflicts with Your Mentor

IN INFORMAL MENTORING relationships, conflict resolution will most likely proceed in line with the overall tone and nature of the relationship. Depending on the length and closeness of the relationship there may be more or less incentive to resolve conflicts in a productive manner. It will rarely be to your benefit to simply abandon the relationship or to make an enemy of your former mentor, but it may not always be to your benefit to make extreme compromises or resource commitments to maintain the relationship. These decisions will depend on the quality and nature of the relationship.

In a situation involving conflict with a formal supervisor, whether or not she is also one of your mentors, you may have to worry more about relationship maintenance due to the fact that you may not be able to end the relationship and move on to another one. In these cases, you may find yourself investing a lot of energy in conflict management. Our general advice on this topic shouldn't surprise you: remain professional and don't let things get personal or otherwise out of hand.

Many conflicts are the result of misunderstandings or poor communication. If you can identify the source of the problem and address it instead of engaging in conflict over fault or blame, you can preempt many conflict situations. Some conflict will arise if your personality type or work style are vastly different from your supervisor's. In these instances you may find that you can improve your working relationship by being more flexible in your work style and making special efforts to accommodate your supervisor. When efforts to prevent conflict do not succeed, you should address the conflict in a professional manner; this means you should deal directly with your supervisor and avoid office gossip and airing your complaints to other employees. You should focus on solving the problem, not on being "right," and be willing to take responsibility for decisions you make and any errors in judgment you may have committed. Digging in your heels and taking the moral high ground may add drama to the work day, but it is rarely a professional solution to an office conflict.

One of the hardest things about office conflict can be the way in which our emotions get involved and threaten to take over. For example, what originates as a disagreement over a report you have prepared can start to feel like an argument over whether you know how to do your job. Suddenly you feel defensive and blame your boss instead of accepting blame yourself. This can all happen in a matter of seconds and without so much as a conscious thought on your part. This is when you need to focus on the practical question at hand and remember that, in many cases, disagreements about work-related issues can be confined to their specific situations. When you are dealing with something more broad, like a personality conflict or a clear disagreement about professional expectations, there may be more room to look at where you stand within the conflict. But even in these instances, stepping back from an emotional response to the situation can help keep conflict in check.

We will discuss conflict, and some options for managing it, in much greater detail in Chapter Eight.

Conflict is an inevitable part of relational life. Whenever two people's interests or motivations are different, there is the potential for conflict. The goal is not always to eliminate or even reduce conflict, but simply to manage it in a constructive way. As communication students, we can use what we know about power and affiliation to come up with constructive ways of dealing with conflict in the workplace.

Summary

IN THIS CHAPTER, WE HAVE discussed some different styles of mentoring and some of the challenges you can face in working with mentors or supervisors. Of course, you should keep in mind that every mentor, and every work situation, is different, and you will need to apply these principles in a context-specific way. We hope, however, that the ideas we have provided and the issues we have discussed will aid in your efforts to build constructive, positive relationships with your mentors.

Review Questions

1. What kind of mentoring style does my mentor practice? How can I tell?

2. What kind of mentoring style do I prefer? What experiences have I had with different mentoring styles that contribute to my preference?

3. What should I do if I am given more work than I can handle?

For Further Reading

Bullis, C., & Bach, B. W. (1989). Are mentor relationships helping organizations? An exploration of developing mentee-mentor-organizational identifications using turning point analysis. *Communication Quarterly, 37*, 199-213.

Shea, G. F. (1999). *Making the most of being mentored*. Menlo Park, CA: Crisp Publications.

Waldeck, J., Oggero, V. O., Plax, T. G., & Kearney, P. (1997). Graduate student/faculty mentoring relationships: Who gets mentored, how it happens, and to what end. *Communication Quarterly, 45*, 93-109.

Chapter Five

Professional Development

W HILE SOME OF YOU may already be familiar with what it is like to work in a professional environment, many of you will use your internship to enter this environment for the first time. Whether you are a seasoned veteran of the employment game or a relative newcomer, there are some important aspects of professional development that you ought to be aware of. This chapter is intended to expose you to a number of these topics and to provide some basic knowledge that may help you deal with issues that arise. Many of the topics addressed in this chapter, such as employment discrimination, sexual harassment, and questions of confidentiality, may seem like things you will never have to deal with. However, these concerns are important to companies and organizations of all types and sizes, so even if you don't have to deal with them directly, they are likely to affect your career in one way or another. In addition, you may find that the advice or suggestions provided in this chapter seem like basic common sense—if so, that's good, because situations arising in these areas will probably require you to make educated, and hopefully insightful, judgment calls about how to proceed.

Professional Dress and Demeanor

IF THERE IS ONE THING THAT YOU will get tired of hearing as you prepare to enter the professional work place, it's that you only get one chance to make a good first impression. This cliché will follow you as you prepare for every future job interview, board presentation, or sales pitch. Of course, it's not as if first impressions are only an issue during specific, identifiable events. In fact, as you probably already know, we are constantly meeting new people and developing new relationships. And, even after you've made a good first impression, you continue to build and alter relationships with the people who know you. What this means for your professional development is that you're never really "done" putting your best foot forward.

Whether you are preparing for a job interview or simply considering your wardrobe for the year, clothing will play an important role in how you will be perceived. Of course, for some industries and professions clothing will matter more—or will matter in a different way—than in others. That is why the best general advice anyone can give you on how to "dress for success" is to know your environment. Know your industry, your company/organization, and know your place within the larger structures. For instance, if you are going to work in advertising you may find that fashion expectations are different than those in political consulting.

Apart from the general advice about knowing your place in the overall professional environment, there are a few other basic suggestions that can be made about dressing for your career. First, for your job interviews, in almost all cases it's better to err on the side of the conservative and formal. One suggestion is to dress as if you were applying for the job *just above* the one you actually hope to get. This advice can also be applied to dressing once you have the first job because then you have to begin dressing so that you will be able to advance. Some image consultants advise people to dress for the job they *want* instead of the one they currently have (Thourlby, 1978). However, be careful not to *over*dress to an extent that alienates your peers or makes you seem too much out of place (Hamilton & Parker, 1997).

Professional demeanor is an additional concern under the notion of making a good first impression. Once again, the best and simplest advice is to identify and comply with the norms of your profession and your organization. Long

It is difficult to overestimate the importance of a good first impression. Remember that you only get one chance to make one!

lunches may be the norm at one organization and may be looked down on at another. Clients may expect phone calls to be returned within 24 or 48 hours. Internal hierarchies may dictate who is on a first-name basis and who is expected to use formal titles. All of these things, and a host of others like them, can affect how you are perceived as a professional. While they may seem insignificant, they are important because they relate to how well you fit into the culture in which you are operating. This fitting in—the ability to comply with the expectations of your job site—is actually at the heart of professional-

ism. After all, a profession is essentially a group of people who share common training, expertise, and standards. So, while no one expects you to give up your sense of individual identity completely— you need to be aware that "fitting in" is part of almost any job, and the choices you make with regard to things like sharing organizational culture may affect your career.

Several general principles can provide a good starting point for cultivating a professional demeanor. The items on this list should seem like common sense to you. Treat your peers *and* your subordinates

with respect. Be on time. Be prepared for meetings and presentations. Learn to give and accept constructive feedback. If you make a mistake, take responsibility for it and try to be proactive about fixing it. Meet deadlines. If you realize that you cannot meet a deadline, be up front about it in advance and seek an alternative arrangement. Depending on your other life experiences, these last four can be the hardest to adjust to as you leave college and enter a full-time profession and, therefore, we'll discuss these issues of time management next.

Managing Time (Yours and Others')

AS WE DISCUSSED ABOVE, meeting deadlines is likely to be an important part of your professional demeanor. Even if you work in an area where there are very few deadlines, at some point someone will expect you to meet a few of them. Of course deadlines are just one aspect of what it means to be employed—even absent the pressure of deadlines, everyone is expected to accomplish a certain quantity of work. This means that time management is important for any job position (and some more than others).

As students (and instructors), we all develop habits or practices that apply to our schoolwork, extracurricular activities, and employment obligations. So, the switch from student life to professional life does not have to be a big one when it comes to time management. However, if your time management techniques leave you frequently racing to meet deadlines and having to cut corners in order to get things done on time,

then you will need to cultivate new ways of managing your work. Using calendars and planners (electronic or the old-fashioned paper kind) can help. Setting internal deadlines that break projects up into smaller tasks that can be more easily accomplished can also be useful.

ate but also wise to refuse to take on additional work. Sometimes mentors, supervisors, or even slightly more experienced peers within your organization can help you negotiate this aspect of your professional development. In addition, if you find yourself in over

If your time management techniques frequently leave you racing to meet deadlines and having to cut corners, it is time to cultivate new ways to manage your workload.

One important thing to learn is how to recognize when your plate is full and how to decline new projects tactfully. While it may seem like a good idea at the time, taking on more work than you can efficiently handle may not be a smart move in the long run. Of course, knowing when and how to decline work comes with professional experience; just be aware that there are times when it is not only appropri-

your head, it is better to speak up as soon as you recognize the problem. Don't wait until you've missed a deadline to tell someone that you are behind; if you step up to the plate in advance, you may find that help is available or that work can be re-prioritized to help you manage the load.

Another piece of advice when it comes to time management:

remember that you do not work in isolation. Your schedule may be fairly autonomous, or you may find that your work relies heavily on that of other people. In the latter case, it will be easy to see how other people's time management skills can affect your life. Being flexible with people who have different approaches to time management is an important part of learning to be a professional. However, you have to keep your eyes open to the fact that someone, somewhere, is responsible for getting the work done. If that person is you, then you need to develop ways to be sure that other people don't create conditions that make it impossible for you to do your job effectively. A big part of managing these situations is simply following up on things: don't just send an e-mail requesting information and then wait while your deadline approaches and no response is forthcoming. Don't assume that your colleague will remember the request you made while waiting for the elevator on your way to lunch. While you don't want to cross the line between being efficient and being irritating, keeping in touch with people about what you are doing for them and what they can do for you helps prevent serious scheduling problems.

If the other person involved is a peer, you may not have the direct authority to set deadlines or impose consequences if deadlines are not met. In these cases, strong people skills are a must. Things like building a sense of shared responsibility and ownership can help. If cooperation does not work, you may have to be more direct and explain that if something cannot be worked out privately, then you will need to speak to a supervisor about the problem. In these extreme cases, be sure you approach the situation in a way that will not put your colleague on the spot; embarrassing a peer is rarely, if ever, a good idea.

Of course, if the person affecting your work/time management is a supervisor, the dynamic of time management may be altered due to the disparity in power. In these cases tact is no less important, and the same sort of cooperative approaches can and should be tried. In many cases supervisory issues with time management are the result of poor communication or inadequate information: your supervisor simply may not know what you have going on, what your deadlines are, and how long things are taking you to complete. In

these cases, frank and constructive feedback (by both parties) can sometimes correct the situation. In other cases, perhaps your supervisor likes to leave things to the last minute and then expects you to "drop everything" to pitch in on the projects once they reach "crisis" mode. Here, you may find yourself in a situation that won't really correct itself (after all, it is a lot to expect that your supervisor will suddenly change his or her working style). In these instances, flexibility on your part may be the best response. However, you should also be mindful of ways to protect yourself from fallout in the event that things get out of hand. Documenting your attempts to get information or materials from other people and keeping track of your communications regarding deadlines and your progress are two simple things that can make your life easier if you ever find yourself having to answer for a missed deadline or a botched timetable.

Knowing and Negotiating the Chain of Command

IN ADDITION TO LEARNING TO manage your time in the context of complex relationships with people at all different levels of the organizational hierarchy, learning the hierarchy itself can be an important part of your first few days and weeks on the job. For instance, there may be times when you have to work with people who are higher up than you but not your direct supervisor. If a problem arises with such a person, do you go directly to him or her? Do you go to your actual boss? When,

if ever, do you go to the other person's boss? Consider what might influence your choice of action: does it depend on what type of problem it is? On how often you have to work with that person? On how well you know his or her boss? Or consider what you would do if your supervisor's direct "boss" (your boss's boss) asks you to do something that exceeds your usual authority. Do you check with your supervisor first? What if you don't check first? Then how do

you handle it if your supervisor becomes upset that she was left out of the loop?

Finally, when are you expected to take problems or concerns you have "up the chain of command" in order to have them addressed? If you feel you must go over someone's head, how do you do it so that you do as little damage as possible to the various relationships that might be affected by such an action? None of these questions is easy, nor does it have a standard answer. Unfortunately, how you handle these situations will depend on the specifics of the relationships involved, your own preferred communication practices, and the environment of your organization. The best, most general advice that we can give you is to be as discrete and professional as you can. Avoid making judgmental accusations about people or their work. As much as possible, stick to the facts and represent these facts in a fair and reasonable way.

There are other issues that may arise with regard to organizational hierarchy. Learning to give constructive feedback to people both above and below you in the hierarchy requires an understanding of the power dynamics at work in each situation. Balancing the personal relationships that may develop with a person you also share a supervisor/supervisee relationship may also become problematic should it become necessary for one of you to "pull rank" in a professional context. Sometimes the problem will arise not out of any one relationship you have at work, but out of the combination of relationships you must maintain and manage at one time. For instance, if you report to two different supervisors or receive work assignments from more than one person, you may find yourself in a situation re-quiring you to prioritize between two or more people, all of whom outrank you. In these instances you need to address problems, such as work overload or conflicting information or expectations concerning your work, very carefully. As in many of the situations addressed here and throughout this book, your good communication skills can help you find ways to raise and solve potential problems in a productive way.

Following Company Policy (Some Special Cases)

MANY ISSUES RELATED TO professionalism and time management simply have to be dealt with from a "learn-by-doing" process. Other issues may be addressed at least in part through reference to explicit organizational policies. Larger organizations, and many smaller ones, have written policies concerning such things as dress codes, intra-office dating, performance evaluations, and employee grievances. Obviously, anytime a written policy exists that relates to your situation, it should be consulted and followed. Most new-employee orientations include a cursory introduction to company policy. If yours does not, simply ask your supervisor or a personnel representative for a copy of the employee handbook or company policy manual. In the event that your organization does not have a set of written policies, take some time to explore with your supervisor or someone in administration the informal procedures used to address employee concerns.

Apart from general "housekeeping" policies, there are two areas where it is particularly important to know your organization's formal and informal policies: confidentiality and workplace discrimination or harassment. While a textbook is not an adequate forum for exploring all of the potential implications of these policies in any depth, we can highlight potential areas of concern for you.

Certain professions impose obligations of confidentiality on their members. Whether these obligations are codified (as in the case of lawyers) or contractual (as in the case of explicit agreements to maintain trade secrets), you need to be familiar with your organization's policies and practices concerning such things as discussing business matters in public places; taking documents or files out of the office; discussing the work you are doing for clients with non-employees; or discussing your organization's business strategies with outsiders.

In addition to these issues of confidentiality from the outside world, you may also be faced with questions of internal confidentiality. In some circumstances you may become privy to information that a colleague (peer, subordinate, or superior) asks you to "keep to yourself." In many instances—such as personal gossip—maintaining the secret will not pose an ethical problem. However, there may be instances where maintaining this sort of internal confidentiality places your organization at risk. One such instance involves allegations of sexual harassment or other forms of workplace discrimination.

Sometimes the best teacher is experience. You will learn to deal with many professional situations effectively just by going through them.

In today's business environment, workplace discrimination (particularly issues dealing with sexual harassment) is a topic that most people are aware of and sensitive to. In addition, more and more organizations of varying sizes are implementing written policies prohibiting discrimination and outlining procedures for addressing problematic situations. This is where knowing and following company policy may become personally difficult. If you become privy to informal allegations of workplace discrimination that are being made by someone in a position subordinate to you, what is your obligation to your company to report these matters? What if the person making the allegations specifically asks you not to report them to people higher up in the organization? What if the alleged harasser/discriminator is your supervisor? On a very practical note, you should know that in some cases your knowledge of the allegations *may* be imputed to your organization and *may* cause the organization to face civil liability if the allegations were to lead to a lawsuit. From a more personal, communicative perspective, allegations of this kind can damage relationships (both personal and professional) and derail careers. Obviously, handling such allegations with tact, sensitivity, and professionalism is necessary, whether you choose to report them to higher authorities or not.

Knowing your organization's policy on sexual harassment and other forms of workplace discrimination is also important so you can protect your rights in the event that you are ever subjected to questionable treatment or accused of inappropriate behavior. Many legal remedies, whether through government agencies or through the courts, will take into consideration whether the person alleging discrimination took steps to follow his or her organization's grievance policy. As a victim of allegedly discriminatory treatment, skipping over internal channels for redress can hurt your chances for securing compensation or other remedies through the law. Finally, if you feel that you have been discriminated against, be sure you understand the requirements of the state and federal agencies that enforce anti-discrimination laws. These agencies have complicated reporting and investigative procedures that must be followed, and there are many deadlines and timetables to be aware of. If you must pursue matters beyond the scope of internal redress, then educate yourself as to your rights and your obligations under the relevant state and federal law. A useful Web site to consult on this matter is the EEOC's site, which is located at http://www.eeoc.gov/index.html.

This discussion is not intended to make you hypersensitive to issues of discrimination or to the complicated legal arena in which many of these issues play themselves out. Instead it is intended to remind you of the value of clear, direct, and productive communication. As students of human communication we know that differences in culture, gender, age, geographic background, and education (to name just a few) can affect how people make meaning out of the messages they receive. Your knowledge of the subtleties of the communication process can potentially help you resolve workplace issues involving a variety of social/personal differences without the need for drastic measures such as a lawsuit. Being aware of areas of potential conflict or concern can help you bring your communication skills into practice in a timely and effective way.

Groups: Participation and Leadership

ANYONE WHO HAS TAKEN A CLASS in small group communication knows that groups are complicated entities with complex dynamics that can either add to group productivity or stand in the way of it. Many career paths will require you to work in small groups of one kind or another along the way. Understanding when and how to employ different group problem solving techniques and being able to identify the symptoms and predictors of groupthink are two areas where having a little expertise can come in handy.

The basic group problem solving procedure has been discussed at length elsewhere (Hamilton & Parker, 1997). It is important to realize that the "basic" model is far from simple and requires a fair amount of skill on the part of the group leader in order to be effective. A well prepared group approaches its task methodically, carefully defining the problem to be solved, researching topics or ideas that need clarification or exploration before a solution can be found, generating adequate criteria for evaluation solutions, and then proceeding to the creative generation of possible solutions (Hamilton & Parker, 1997). While problems can arise at any point throughout the process, the generation of creative solutions may be the area where proper training in small group techniques is most helpful. During the solution generation stage, it is important to focus on generating as many ideas as possible—to do this the group should avoid negative feedback during the generation process. If the group attempts to perform the next step—solution evaluation—while generating ideas then creative possibilities may be limited (Hamilton & Parker, 1997). Because group problem solving requires the generation of ideas within a group, we have listed some of the common techniques that a group can use to produce ideas and alternatives. A few of these techniques are listed in Figure 5.1.

Beyond the danger of shutting down creative possibilities too quickly in the problem-solving stage, small groups also face the danger of *groupthink*. Groupthink is a phenomenon that occurs when a group adopts an uncritical way of thinking in order to avoid conflict within the group (Hamilton & Parker, 1997). This process generally leads groups to make less constructive decisions than those produced by groups who employ critical thinking. Since one of the

---

Figure 5.1

Group Techniques for Generating Ideas

Brainstorming: A method for generating lists of creative alternatives. This technique can be used at various points in the problem-solving process to generate solutions, criteria, and topics for research. To be successful, a brainstorming session should follow these guidelines:

- Focus on encouraging spontaneous and open participation. Avoid negative feedback or evaluative comments.

- Generate the longest list of alternatives possible. Again, this is not the time to evaluate potential solutions or to begin thinking about what will or will not work out.

- Be creative! Once you turn off your evaluative mind-set, be sure to let your creativity take over. Ideas that seem completely crazy may contain kernels of inspiration that lead to workable alternatives.

- Build from ideas that have already been offered. This is a group activity! If you have established an environment in which people are comfortable throwing out ideas without fear of negative feedback, then it should be easy to take one idea and run with it in a number of possible directions.

Nominal Group Technique (NGT): This alternative generation technique has some advantages over brainstorming. Because it is set up to let group members generate ideas on their own, it can eliminate some of the pressures that may be associated with speaking out in a group. The basic procedure for NGT is:

- First, each group member writes down ideas on his or her own, without discussion.

- Next, everyone's ideas are listed on a chalkboard in a round robin procedure, in which each person puts forward one idea at a time until everyone's ideas are listed. This equalizes the opportunity for each member to have his or her ideas brought before the group. Discussion is kept to a minimum at this point.

- Finally, each member selects a designated number of ideas that appeal to him or her and ranks them in order of preference. These rankings are then tabulated for each idea. The idea emerging with the most votes (the highest rankings) is the most popular idea.

Brainwriting: This is a combination technique in which each member generates ideas on his or her own and the ideas are then passed around to the other members. As members exchange ideas, they have a chance to build on pre-existing ideas or to add new ideas to each list. This has the benefit of allowing for shared creativity without imposing the pressure of speaking out to the group. At the end of a designated time period, the lists are collected and the ideas are evaluated by the group as a whole.

Figure 5.2

Characteristics of Groupthink

Groupthink is a phenomenon that occurs in small groups when the focus shifts from effective problem solving to a desire to avoid internal group conflict and maintain group harmony. Hamilton and Parker (1997) list several symptoms of groupthink, a few of which are listed below.

The illusion of invulnerability and illusion of morality. Because a group experiencing groupthink stops thinking critically it may come to believe that any decision it makes has to be the right one. This has two components. First, it can lead to the illusion of invulnerability, which makes the group feel that "nothing can go wrong" with their chosen course of action and can lead the group to make risky decisions because they do not effectively evaluate the risks involved. In addition, it can lead to the illusion of group morality, which makes the group feel that whatever it chooses to do is necessarily a good and moral choice. This may lead the group to ignore possible negative consequences of its decision. Groups suffering from the illusion of morality may fail to ask the questions: "What will happen in the long run if we do this?" "How might this decision have a negative effect on the community, the environment, or our employees?"

Shared stereotypes. The group may latch onto, or even create, stereotypes that explain away ideas, opinions, beliefs, or information that contradict the majority opinion within the group. In this way, the group can discount the stereotype instead of actually addressing the merits of the conflicting position. For example, if the organization's General Counsel has advised against a certain course of action, a group experiencing groupthink may adopt the shared stereotype that "lawyers are too paranoid about being sued" in order to justify ignoring the advice.

Rationalization. Like shared stereotypes, rationalization works to justify the group's actions without critically considering opposing positions or alternate courses of action. This behavior inhibits critical thinking and compromises the quality of the group's overall problem solving process.

Self-censorship. In a groupthink situation, it may begin to appear that everyone agrees. In these cases, group members who disagree may censor their opinions and keep quiet. They do this because the group's values have shifted to place an emphasis on the group's internal harmony. Members of a group experiencing groupthink are more likely to "go along" with group decisions.

primary benefits to be gained from making decisions in small groups is to improve the quality of the solutions, groupthink undermines the value of the group process extensively. Listed in Figure 5.2 are some of the characteristics of groupthink.

Your Internship and Your Career

WHEN YOUR INTERNSHIP IS OVER, you will hopefully realize that you have learned a lot from this experience. Perhaps you have acquired a variety of skills and knowledge about the field of work your internship involves and find yourself well poised to begin a career in that area. Maybe you've simply formed rewarding relationships with co-workers and your mentor. Alternatively, you may have learned exactly what you don't want in a future job or supervisor. In fact, more than one of these possibilities is probably true for you. Whatever the case, we hope you are beginning to realize that an internship is a developmental experience from which you will draw for many years an important part of your career development. Upon graduation, many former interns accept full-time positions at the same company. Many others hear about job opportunities and receive references and recommendations from former internship contacts. In their first post-graduation jobs, most will draw upon and expand the skills that were developed during coursework and internship experiences.

At some point after you start your first job, you'll have to consider what comes next. For some job positions there is a natural progression already established that lays out a possible career path for you. In other instances, your first job may not lead to an obvious next step. Whether you are working toward a promotion within a department, a lateral move into another field or department, or a move to a higher position in the same field, eventually you will find yourself thinking about improving—or simply changing—the job you're in. You may want better pay or benefits. Maybe you will be looking for increased responsibility or other ways to challenge yourself.

Perhaps you will be seeking a different work environment or corporate culture. These are all valid reasons for making a move. The idea here is not to rush you into premature speculation about when or why you might look to change jobs. Instead the idea is to address some concerns that you will want to keep in mind throughout your career. From your first day on the job to your last, your professional advancement is something you can always think about.

Many of the things we've talked about in this chapter will help you do a good job and, just as important, make good impressions. These two things go a long way toward making sure that when the time comes you will be promotable within your organization or marketable outside of it. In addition to doing a good job, you need to consider how you document all of your good work. This means that you will want to take opportunities to perform self-evaluations very seriously. Self-evaluations are a chance to put forward your best qualities while honestly assessing your weaker areas and setting goals for change; you can use these exercises to demonstrate your maturity and potential for growth as well as to highlight your existing qualities and achievements. Relatedly, when you receive a performance review from your supervisor or mentor you should take that opportunity to seek suggestions for how you can improve your overall performance. Use these reviews as a source of valuable information about what you need to be doing more of (or less of). You may have to be willing to speak up if there are negative aspects of the review that you disagree with. Obviously, not every review will be negotiable, but

in some instances you can address content that is less favorable than you like either in conversation or in written form. In some instances having an honest conversation about perceived problems with your work can put you in a position to explain or clarify misunderstandings or inaccurate perceptions. Even if the negative material remains in the review you can have the benefit of clarifying the perceived problems in your work and identify specific ways to address those problems.

In addition to formal reviews, keep copies of less formal correspondence you might receive that reflects well on your work. These items can provide you with reminders of specific instances, events, and projects that you might want to highlight in future conversations about your work performance. You may find that, when you ask a supervisor to recommend you for a promotion, it is useful to be able to point to particular times when you were praised for your good work. No one likes a bragger, but a certain amount of healthy self-promotion can aid in your efforts to advance.

Of course, if you ever receive feedback that indicates that you need to improve certain aspects of your performance, it will be important that you handle the situation professionally. While you should not be afraid to speak up if you feel that you are being unfairly criticized, you have to be mature enough to accept constructive criticism and to admit when you need to improve your performance. You may find that accepting negative evaluations of your work in a professional and results-oriented manner can go a long way toward offsetting any negative impact that the weak performance issues might have had. Proving yourself to be able to learn from mistakes, set and achieve personal goals, and take responsibility for your shortcomings is an important way to earn people's trust and respect.

We commented above that you should dress for the job you want. This general advice is also something to keep in mind when you consider how to do your job. While you must not overstep your authority or the limits of your knowledge or ability, you should be willing to take on new responsibilities and learn new tasks. You can't assume that your supervisor or other managers in your organization will automatically know when you are ready to expand your responsibilities or learn something new. A certain amount of initiative is required on your part. If you are willing to step outside your comfort zone and push yourself a little, you will make yourself more valuable to your organization and more promotable in the future.

Summary

WHEN IT COMES TO DEVELOPING yourself as a professional, there is a lot to keep in mind. In this chapter we've discussed some of the basic issues, including appearance, demeanor, time management, and knowing how to follow company policy and the chain of command. As with the other advice we've given you in this book, you will need to adapt these principles to your specific work situations. To the extent that you are conscientious of these and other issues of professional development, however, you will better prepare yourself to succeed in the working world.

Review Questions

1. Why is it important to dress and behave professionally at all times?

2. What kinds of company policies do I need to be familiar with?

3. What should I do if I believe I have been the victim of workplace discrimination?

4. Have I witnessed or experienced any of the symptoms or negative effects of groupthink during your internship? If so, how have they manifested themselves in the way people communicate in my workplace? If not, what is it about the way people in the organization communicate that prevents the emergence of groupthink?

For Further Reading

Evans, G. (2000). *Play like a man: Win like a woman.* New York: Broadway Books.

Malloy, J. T. (1988). *New dress for success.* New York: Warner Books, Inc.

Malloy, J. T. (1996). *New women's dress for success.* New York: Warner Books.

Solomon, D. H., & Williams, M. L. M. (1997). Perceptions of social-sexual communication at work: The effects of message, situation, and observer characteristics on judgments of sexual harassment. *Applied Communication Research, 25,* 196-216.

Trethewey, A. (1999). Disciplined bodies: Women's embodied identities at work. *Organization Studies, 20,* 423-450.

Chapter Six

Writing for the Workplace

THE ABILITY TO communicate effectively in writing is one of the most important professional skills you can develop. Although few people would claim to be experts in grammar and syntax, most people can remember a time when they struggled to make sense of a written text. In situations involving personal letters, family recipes, or directions to a party, a lack of clarity is frustrating, but we are usually able to use context, personal knowledge, and common sense to effectively muddle through. In professional situations readers rarely have the time, background information and contextual clues, or personal motivation necessary to invest excessive energy in making *useful* sense out of a poorly written document. Ultimately, written communications that burden the reader too much often fail to do their job. In fact, poorly written documents may create *mis-*communications, actually working against their intended purpose.

Making the transition from "writing for school" to "writing for work" may require you to pay attention to aspects of your writing that you have previously ignored or taken for granted. All too often, students faced with a course-related writing assignment focus on the details of an assignment prompt and the instructor's grading criteria when approaching and completing the assignment. This makes some sense in the context of a graded assignment; however, reliance on overtly stated, and frequently artificial, criteria for a paper can lead to a sense that writing is a mechanical process focused on "getting by" and "getting done." Of course, it is important to be able to follow instructions, identify and meet expectations, and accomplish what you are asked to do. But the somewhat artificial nature of graded writing assignments does not compare to the more dynamic and diverse nature of writing tasks you will face in the workplace. Your workplace writing will rarely present itself in the form of a clearly stated prompt, complete with suggested topics and length requirements. Workplace writing will require you to carefully consider your objectives, your audience's needs and expectations, and your available resources. While certain types of workplace writings do have fairly standard formats and purposes, these standards operate merely as guidelines, not hard and fast rules. Learning to apply general guidelines, like those explored below, is a large part of becoming an efficient and effective workplace writer.

Make Efficient Use of Your Time

ONE OF THE MOST IMPORTANT aspects of workplace writing is learning to allocate and manage your time. In a perfect world, you would have as much time as you needed to complete each writing task. But as you have already learned from your experiences in school, this is rarely the case. In fact, there will be occasions when you have little advance warning that a task is coming and very little control over how much time you have to complete it. This means that you need to do your best to plan the things you can plan and actively manage the writing tasks that you do have control over.

Part of actively managing your writing tasks is setting realistic expectations for how much you can accomplish in a given period of time. Underestimating how long something will take to complete can lead to problems—in order to meet a deadline that comes too quickly, you may be tempted to cut corners on the writing/revising portion of the project. In school, the decision to stay up all night and write the paper you have been researching for three weeks may result in a slightly lower grade. In the workplace, the same writing strategy may result in your superior, colleagues, and clients thinking less of your professional ability and competence. Take it from us, no instructor likes to read a paper that is poorly organized, has numerous grammatical errors, and is inadequately developed. But we can also assure you that a boss or client will appreciate these errors even less, and may form opinions or make decisions based on the

Learning to write well takes time and practice, but the effort will pay off in many ways during your internship and your professional career.

written product that have more lasting consequences than a poor grade.

Early in your career you will encounter writing tasks that are new to you. This may make estimating an appropriate timeframe for completion more difficult. When possible, consult with your supervisor or colleagues at the beginning of the project to determine if they can provide you with guidelines. Keep in mind, however, that a task may take you longer to complete the first few times you do it; so if an experienced employee suggests that a week is enough time to complete a project, you may want to give yourself a little more time. Of course, how long you have to complete a project may be largely or wholly determined by the needs of the client or some larger project schedule. Be sure you determine up front when the final product is due and whether this deadline is firm or flexible.

Communicating regularly with your supervisor, client, or team-members about your progress and any unexpected problems or delays can help you in a number of ways. First, these interim discussions can keep you on track and encourage you to work steadily toward your goal, instead of putting things off. Next, touching base along the way can help correct problems or misunderstandings before they cost too much time and energy. Sometimes these interim progress reviews can help you re-prioritize your efforts, narrow the scope of a problem that turns out to be bigger than expected, and help you develop a more thorough understanding of what is expected of you and your work. Finally, if you have kept your audience informed of your progress and the potential obstacles you face, you may find that delivering "bad news"—in the event of either a missed deadline or unexpectedly

unfavorable content—is a little easier.

Many people struggle to make progress on writing projects because they expect to create a "perfect" document in one try. However, many of the most productive and successful writers go through several drafts before arriving at a finished product. That means you should not expect, for example, that one sentence will need to be perfect before moving to the next one. Instead, it is probably more realistic for you assume that each project will be completed through a cycle of writing, reviewing, revising, proofreading, then reviewing, revising, proofreading, and so on. Don't be discouraged if your first few of drafts are quite "rough."

Do Your Homework

PART OF WRITING A GOOD course paper is doing the research necessary to support your claims and guide your analysis. Although your workplace writing tasks may not send you off to the library to pour over research journals, you will be expected in many instances to locate, analyze, and evaluate information from a variety of sources. The same skills you use in your library research can help you with the research you must do on the job.

In addition to gathering the information you might need to complete your task, you also need to be sure you understand who your audience will be, what the purpose of your writing is, how the writing will be used, and by whom. This means

Sometimes people struggle with writing projects because they try to create a perfect document on the first try. Writing is a process; give yourself time to let your writing evolve.

asking questions and clarifying the context in which you are working. You may want to find out if your employer has a standard format for internal and/or external memos. If there is no established standard, ask to review a few examples of similar documents that your supervisor or colleagues have produced in the past. Ask whether your primary audience has particular expectations or preferences with regard to document format, length, or delivery method.

No matter what your audience or purpose, you must leave yourself enough time to actually formulate the content of your document. Often, time constraints force us to produce written products quickly and without careful planning. This will be true in the workplace—no matter how carefully we plan. However, you need to strike a balance between gathering information, analyzing the material you have, and finally producing your document. Rushing any one of these aspects of the writing process can lead to a poor product. Especially when you are performing an analysis or evaluation upon which other people will rely when making decisions, it is important to think through your position and conclusions thoroughly. If you feel that your analysis or decision-making process was hurried due to time constraints, or was otherwise limited (e.g., by a lack of information or an incomplete set of decision-making criteria) be sure you discuss this with the person(s) to whom you are delivering the final product. It may

even be appropriate to note the limitations you faced in the text itself. Of course, you do not want to be seen as making excuses for poor work or for a less-than-thorough effort; the limitations we are referring to here are those that were outside your control and significant enough to have an effect on your work.

As you can probably guess, there is often a close connection between managing your time and doing your homework. You may find that as you delve deeper into a project your initial time estimates

need to be revised. You may discover, as you consult with your supervisor or client during an interim meeting, that the document you planned to present as an internal memo really needs to be a letter to the stockholders or a press release. Unlike the requirements for course papers, professional writing projects often change over time. This leads us to a brief discussion of two things that you must always keep your eye on: your objectives and the details.

Keep Your Eye on the Right Objectives

As a young lawyer, one of this book's authors (Michele) faced some problems in her workplace writing. The objective for the basic legal memo is to identify essential points of law and the ways in which these points applied to the particular facts of the case at hand. This requires a good deal of weeding-out: weeding-out cases and legal principles that are different from the case at hand, weeding-out facts in the case at hand that do not need further development. Accustomed to the more academic style of writing used in scholarly law review articles, Michele wanted each memo to be a thorough survey of every aspect of the relevant law. Instead of quickly focusing on the principles and facts that could make or break her particular case, Michele wanted

to explore the nuances and details of the law in general. Unfortunately, few clients want to pay for extra research just to "know" a little bit (or a lot) more about the law.

When you are faced with a writing task at work, whether it's a letter, a memo, or a press release, you should always clearly identify exactly what you need to accomplish through that task. Are you writing for a very specific audience, a more general public, or merely documenting things for a file so that someone who comes along later will have the information he or she needs? If you are writing for an audience other than the file, do you need to inform, persuade, motivate, praise, or criticize them? What action or result do you hope

will take place as a result of your writing? Do you need the audience to take a particular action or merely understand the material presented? You may find that you have to present the same material in different ways, depending on whether you are briefing your immediate supervisor on the status of a project that has fallen behind schedule or motivating your staff to meet the necessary deadlines to get the project back on track. Questions of audience and purpose cannot be overlooked if you want to attain the results you need.

Keep Your Eye on the Details

We have talked broadly about workplace writing as a process that must be actively managed and carefully directed toward a specified objective in order to be fully effective. Apart from these general principles that can help you think about

your writing tasks in a way that makes them more productive, we can also share some practical advice that can help you deliver a higher quality written product. By keeping your eye on the following details, you can enhance your ef-

fectiveness and credibility as a business communicator.

ORGANIZATION. You may not write many five-paragraph papers in the workplace, but you will still need to present your ideas and information in a way that helps your reader to follow along. A clean, well conceived structure can enhance the effectiveness of your communication (this is true of written as well as verbal communication). On the other hand, writing that jumps around, fails to clearly establish connections between topics, includes incomplete thoughts or poorly developed ideas, or fails to demonstrate a logical progression from beginning to end will often leave the reader uninformed, unconvinced, and unimpressed.

There is no one right way to organize a business document. Certain simple documents, like cover letters, letters or inquiry, or standardized reports within a company, may follow an easily identifiable template. Other documents will have to be organized around the particularities of that writing task. You will be best served if you do your homework—complete your research, identify the audience and objectives of the document, and spend adequate time formulating your ideas and analysis—before you try to force the document to take a particular form. Content and purpose should have the primary role in dictating how the text should look.

One way to enhance the organization of your writing projects is to use headings and bullets or numerical outlines to visually reinforce the logical structure that you have chosen for your material. When used effectively, headings can break up the flow of the text, providing the reader with a signpost that signals a change in topics. In complicated texts, with many nested issues and topics, the use of headings and subheadings can help the reader keep track of what has been said and what to expect. Similarly, the use of bullets or numbering systems can introduce important topics that the reader should be looking for later on, emphasize the inter-relatedness

of items on a list, or just draw the eye to important information that might otherwise get lost in the larger body of text. Of course, the use of these organizational devices is no substitute for a clear, logical, organizational structure within the material itself. Formatting with headings and bullets can help you reinforce a logical transition between ideas or emphasize certain parts of your text, but formatting will not help the reader make sense of a text that lacks cohesion or fails to provide adequate support for its conclusions.

LANGUAGE, TONE, AND CONTENT. When writing for the workplace you should use language that is direct, clear, and appropriate. Avoid contractions and the use of slang. Also be careful only to use words that you fully understand and can use properly. There is no practical reason to rely on overly complicated sentence structures or "fancy sounding" words; these often make it more difficult for your reader to understand and follow your discussion. Of course, selecting the appropriate language for your writing also includes using correct grammar and following standard punctuation rules. In-

stead of viewing compliance with these rules as an additional, unappealing task or a limitation on your personal style of writing, try looking at this compliance as a tool for more effective communication. You do not have to be an expert to use simple, clean sentence structures and employ punctuation in an effective way. Observing the basics of good grammar and syntax will increase the readability and effectiveness of your writing immensely. This is an instance when a little effort can make a large difference in the quality of the end result.

Your choice of language will affect the clarity of your writing. It will also influence the tone of your writing. Tone is the more subtle quality of a text that reflects many things about the writer and his or her relationship to the reader. Your workplace writing should convey the appropriate attitude toward your audience and your objective. Business writing typically takes a fairly formal tone, one that avoids contradictions, uses personal pronouns carefully and sparingly, and avoids irony, sarcasm, or other easily misunderstood rhetorical devices. However, your writing

Do your homework—complete your research, identify the audience and objectives of the document, and spend adequate time formulating your ideas and analysis—before you try to force the document to take a particular form.

should still remain conversational. That does not mean that you should write like you talk—in fact, most of us speak with a relatively low level of precision and grammatical correctness. Conversational writing is meant to convey a set of qualities (e.g., it is well paced, interesting, directed at the interests of the reader) that make a document easy to read and understand.

Even within business writing you may find different levels of formality appropriate for different situations. Business correspondence will most often require a more formal tone than your personal correspondence, but you may find that long-term business relationships yield slightly less formal letters than those used during initial interactions. In fact, learning to appro-

priately personalize certain types of correspondence is very important. Follow-up letters after interviews or other meetings and thank-you letters for assistance given or favors rendered should be personalized in a way that adds to the sincerity of the letter and increases the likelihood that the person receiving the letter will remember you favorably. One thing you must

---

Figure 6.1

Practical Tips for Effective Business Writing

The tips included in this list are based on the authors' professional experiences and on the advice given in *Webster's New World: Business Writing Book* (Worth, 2002).

1. **Avoid jargon and unnecessarily long or fancy-sounding words**.

   - Worth (2002) gives several examples of how we can substitute conversational language for what he calls "businessese." For instance, do not use "accrue" when you can use "add." Do not say "endeavor" when you can say "try."

   - Your writing should be easy to understand the first time it is read. Use words that make up an "everyday" vocabulary and be sure to use each word in a conventional and accurate way.

2. **Write in the active voice**.

   - Example of passive voice: "The interns were required by their instructor to turn in their contracts."

   - Example of active voice: "The instructor required the interns to turn in their contracts."

3. **Use transitions**.

   - Transitions help your readers keep up. They let them know where you are going with your writing. This makes it easier to follow your reasoning and focus on the substance of your message.

   - Transitions can connect similar ideas ("for example," "in addition"), indicate a contrast or tension ("otherwise," "nevertheless"), or show emphasis ("most important").

4. **Obey standard rules of use**.

   - Subject and verb agreement: The subject and verb in each sentence must agree in number. That is, a singular subject requires the singular form of the verb. Sorting this out requires you to identify the actual subject of your sentence:

     - The internship *class has* a portfolio due. (singular)

     - The *students* in the internship class *have* a portfolio due. (plural)

   - Pronoun and noun agreement: A pronoun must clearly refer to a particular noun and match that noun in number:

     - *Everyone* wants *his or her* job to be fulfilling. ("everyone" is singular)

     - The *magazines* are in *their* usual spot. ("magazines" is plural)

     - Today's *delivery* of oranges was late; *it* arrived after breakfast. ("delivery" is singular)

---

keep in mind when writing a business letter or preparing a document for the workplace is that you cannot control who is going to see it once it leaves your hands. The tone may be appropriate for the intended recipient, but inappropriate for his or her boss, co-workers, or other parties. It is usually best to err on the side of formality. As long as you maintain an otherwise pleasant and professional tone, formality will not be held against you, and it will not come back to haunt you in the event that someone else gets a hold of your letter or memo. For some practical tips and guidelines on how to establish the appropriate language use and tone for business writing, see Figure 6.1.

We have already talked about the importance of doing adequate research and planning for your writing projects. These considerations obviously relate to the content you will produce. Another set of considerations that should shape your content decisions concerns your audience and objectives. Just as you want to choose an effective organizational structure and tone for your writing, you also want to strategically consider the content that you include. Not every project calls for the inclusion of every last detail or a discussion of every topic in equal depth. Decide what

you need your audience to know and then focus on conveying that necessary information. One thing to consider when choosing how much detail or depth to go into is whether the document is for internal or external use. Another consideration is the amount of background information or expertise your audience can be expected to already possess. Finally, take into consideration whether your written product incorporates, or takes a position on, information or ideas that are not commonly accepted. For example, an internal memo to an established project team, whose members are presumed to have a strong understanding of the facts and issues surrounding the memo's content, may not need to re-hash facts and conclusions that have already been established. On the other hand, an internal memo to a project team that includes many new members or a memo that makes certain assumptions about conditions or resources that are not already accepted may need to review the basic facts and issues involved. External memos may be crafted along these same lines, but with the additional consideration of whether there are some things that the external party does not need to know, or should not know, for whatever reason.

PROOFREADING. Proofreading is critical to every writing project you will undertake. Word processing programs can be useful for

checking spelling and identifying certain grammatical problems. However, these programs are no substitute for your own critical eye and careful attention. One useful proofreading exercise is to read your text out loud. This exercise forces you to slow down and pay close attention to the text. Another useful practice is to enlist the help of a colleague who will read your document carefully and provide honest feedback. Proofreading takes time and can be tedious. Because it is done after the text is finished, there is often very little time left for the proofreading process. However, you should try to leave yourself enough time to carefully review it and make necessary corrections. If you have just finished writing a document moments ago, you may not notice your own errors, so if at all possible, you should try to step away from the text for a while to get fresh "eyes" before returning to proofread it. This is another reason why leaving yourself sufficient time to proofread effectively is so important. You may also find it useful to proofread long documents in stages. As you finish a section, stop and do a careful proofreading job. This breaks up the monotony of the process and limits the amount of last minute proofreading you have to rush through right before the deadline.

Some Thoughts about E-mail

ALL OF THE CONSIDERATIONS discussed here apply in some way to the use of electronic mail. It is typical to think of e-mail as being a less formal medium of communication. When we put it to personal use, it often is used very casually and the rules of grammar, syntax, and organization are often relaxed (if not ignored altogether). However, the

use of e-mail in a professional setting should remain fairly formal and structured. Particularly when communicating with your superiors, your clients, and organizations external to your company with whom you conduct business, you should always use professional standards for language, tone, and content. Do not be fooled by its

apparent informality into putting something in an e-mail message that you would not commit to paper or say to someone's face.

Even when dealing with peers, keep in mind that the caveat of not being able to control who sees your message is especially true for e-mail. Not only are e-mail messages themselves easily forwarded or otherwise passed on (whether intentionally or by mistake), but long after the message itself has been deleted from the recipient's inbox and your outbox, there may be ways to retrieve and reconstruct the text.

Summary

LIKE MUCH OF THE ADVICE in this book, the discussion presented here is based on practical experience and common sense. Many of the topics touch upon things you have probably heard from your college instructors with regard to your class assignments. Whether you understood the importance of grammar, organization, or proofreading in your course assignments, you should stop to consider the importance of these things in how you present yourself in the business world. Like it or not, we are all evaluated on our ability to use standard language and write according to certain social expectations. For many of your business associates, your writing will be their primary—and sometimes their only—exposure to you as a professional. Good writing takes time, effort, and attention, but it is worth these investments.

Review Questions

1. What are some considerations that shape the content of a business memo or letter?

2. How do you deal with a situation in which you are having trouble meeting a deadline for a written project?

3. Why do we say that objective and audience should always be kept in mind when writing for the workplace?

4. Formats and guidelines can be useful, but they have limitations. What are these limitations?

5. Should e-mail be treated differently than other workplace writing? Why or why not?

For Further Reading

Pearsall, T. E., Cunningham, D. H., & Smith, E. O. (2002). *How to write for the world of work* (6th ed.). Orlando, FL: Harcourt College Publishers.

Worth, R. (2002). *Webster's new world: Business writing handbook*. Indianapolis: Wiley.

Chapter Seven

Dealing with Some Common Problems on the Job

COMMUNICATION INTERNS work in a variety of locations and for a variety of organizations. Their job responsibilities can vary considerably. However, there are certain challenges that seem to be common across a number of internship situations. Here, we will discuss some of the more common problems that interns face, and provide some advice on how to address these issues, should you ever face them.

My Mentor Never Gets My Paperwork Done in Time

AS YOU GO THROUGH YOUR internship, there will be several occasions during the semester when you must have your mentor complete paperwork for you. This sounds easy enough. However, you will find that mentors are busy people, and it is common for interns to have difficulty getting their mentors to complete various pieces of paperwork for them in time. An example might be your midterm evaluation. You have the form in Appendix B, and you will be told at the beginning of the semester when it is due. If you wait until the day before it's due to give it to your mentor, chances are you will not have it back in time. This applies to all of your paperwork; busy mentors will find it difficult to complete and return your forms if you give them little notice.

Is it your mentor's fault if you turn your paperwork in late? Au contraire! Remember that the responsibility for making your deadlines lies with you. If you turn in your assignments late, it will not be your mentor's grade that suffers, it will be yours. If this sounds harsh, let us assure you that things are no different in the professional world. Ultimately, you will be responsible for things that are assigned to you—and this includes turning in your paperwork by the prescribed deadlines.

So, what is an intern to do if his or her mentor doesn't complete paperwork in a timely fashion? The key is planning. You need to give your mentor ample notice as to when various forms are due, and you need to be aware of his or her schedule and times when he or she will be unavailable. We commonly hear interns say that they could not get their forms completed because their mentors were on vacation when the forms were due. Plan ahead: if your mentor is going to be gone, make sure you approach him or her with your paperwork well in advance. It might also be useful to ask your mentor who else in the organization could complete paperwork in his or her absence; this will allow you to approach someone else if your mentor is unavailable.

My Internship Involves Too Many or Too Few Hours

WHEN YOU BEGAN YOUR internship you agreed, with your mentor, on a total number of hours you would be completing during the semester. This number was based partly on how many credit hours you were taking and partly on your specific interests and work needs. Sometimes, though, interns find that their mentors expect them to work more hours than they originally agreed to, or that there is simply not enough work to fill the required minimum number of hours.

If you find yourself in either of these situations, it is important to address them. In both cases, your first step should be to speak with your mentor. You will want to be clear that your concern is not with the nature of the work or your satisfaction with your mentor, but simply with your ability to work the number of hours that you and your mentor agreed you would work. We know that it can be uncomfortable to bring up issues like these with a mentor; however, it is critical that you do so. Your mentor is the

> *Plan ahead with your mentor to make sure your required paperwork gets done. Remember, getting your assignments completed on time is your responsibility!*

person responsible for overseeing your internship and making decisions about your workload, so he or she is in the best position to resolve problems with your schedule. You might refer back to Chapters Four and Five for tips on time management and on resolving conflicts with your mentor.

If you have addressed the issue with your mentor and find that your situation does not improve as a result, your next step will be to communicate your concerns to the internship director. Often, he or she can provide you with additional advice on handling the situation. In other cases, it may be that the director will contact your mentor and work out an agreement for the rest of your internship.

Someone I Work with Asked Me Out on a Date

ROMANCE IN THE WORKPLACE is a tricky issue, not only because it can be difficult to mix personal and professional relationships with people, but also because romantic advances can constitute sexual harassment under certain conditions. Nevertheless, it is not uncommon for love to blossom at work. What should you do if someone you work with expresses a romantic interest in you?

Should you find yourself in this situation, we recommend that you give thought to at least two issues. First, what are your feelings toward this person? If the interest is not mutual, then it is probably to your advantage to make this clear up-front. Doing so can help to prevent misunderstandings and spare hurt feelings down the road. If this person accepts your position, you can both move on with your work. If he or she continues to make advances toward you (e.g., continually asking you out or commenting on his or her feelings for you) after you have made it clear that such advances are unwelcome, this may necessitate your discussing the situation with your mentor or supervisor.

However, if you find that the attraction is mutual, then you need to learn what your organization's position is on employee dating. Some companies have formal policies restricting employee dating or clarifying the conditions under which it is acceptable. Other organizations may have a position on the issue that is part of the organizational culture, even though it is not codified in writing. In either case, your mentor or personnel manager can give you advice about how to proceed.

All I'm Being Asked to Do Is Clerical Work

MOST INTERNSHIPS, LIKE MOST jobs, will involve some amount of clerical work. However, the goal of the internship program is to help you gain experiences beyond the clerical. This should have been made clear to your mentor at the time you arranged your internship and signed your contract. No matter how carefully you lay out your expectations and the program's requirements to your mentor in advance, you may find yourself doing more clerical work than you expected or agreed to. In these cases, the first thing you should do is speak with your mentor. In a professional but firm manner, revisit your expectations and the internship program's requirements (not more than 20% clerical work). Make sure your mentor knows that you do not mind doing some clerical work (after all, that is part of the entry-level game everyone has to play), but stress the importance of moving beyond those tasks toward more complete professional development. If your mentor feels that his or her only option is to give you clerical work, then you need to address the situation. Sometimes mentors will wait for you to take the initiative to show that you are eager and able to take on more advanced responsibilities, so if you are passively waiting for the good work to come your way, you may be shooting yourself in the foot!

If you have this conversation with your mentor and the situation does not improve, then you should bring your concerns to the internship director. At this time, the director will discuss your situation with you and determine whether he or she needs to intervene.

I Was Offered a Job at Another Company in the Middle of My Internship

BECAUSE YOU ARE NEARING the end of your undergraduate career, you may have begun looking for a full-time job for after college. Sometimes, interns are offered such a position while they are still completing their internships. This poses a quandary: You don't want to turn down the great job you've just been offered, but you're still not finished with your internship.

In this situation, we recommend that you begin by asking your prospective employer (the organization offering you the full-time job) if you can put off starting work until your internship is complete. This may mean increasing the number of hours you work each week at your internship so that you can finish sooner, but if the prospective employer is willing to wait, then you can accomplish both goals. If not, you will need to make a decision whether to accept the job and leave your internship unfinished or to turn down the job and complete your internship. Keep in mind that if you leave your internship before you have completed your minimum hours, then you must withdraw from the internship course or you will most likely receive a failing grade. If the prospective job is good enough, that may be a sacrifice you are willing to make—but be sure to check with your academic advisor first to make certain it wouldn't prevent you from finishing your degree. If you do decide to leave your internship, contact the internship director right away. We will expect you to give as much notice to your internship mentor as you possibly can before leaving.

I Don't Like This Internship at All

ON OCCASION STUDENTS WILL accept an internship that they later find to be less than ideal. Sometimes the problem will arise because of a poor relationship with one or more mentors/supervisors. Sometimes the nature of the work is vastly different from what was expected and the reality is unappealing. In some ways the old saying "hindsight is 20/20" is the best conclusion to be drawn in these situations: No job-hunting experience is perfect and occasionally people make employment choices that work out poorly. In these instances, you hope you learn something about who you are, what you are looking for in a job, and how to ask questions (in advance) that will ensure a better fit in future jobs.

However, given the unique nature of the internship experience, the solution to this problem is a bit more complicated than simply "live and learn." Instead, we urge you to work closely with your mentor to identify and correct any problems that are contributing to your unhappiness. If it is a question of type, quality, or amount of work, you should address these concerns with your mentor in a direct manner. Perhaps your mentor will be able to make some adjustments that can satisfy you. Perhaps an honest conversation with your mentor will help you understand why things are the way they are and will help you adjust your expectations about the work you are doing. Similarly, if you have an unsatisfactory relationship with your mentor, the best solution is to address this problem directly. As we discussed in Chapter Four, people have different styles of mentoring and being mentored; through effective communication people can adapt to each other's needs and preferences if they are willing to be honest and self-reflexive.

We do not believe in the utopian ideal that communication can solve everything, but before you throw up your hands and either resign yourself to having a miserable semester or quitting your internship, we suggest you make a sincere effort at resolving your problems through communication. If the problems are not resolved, or if you are unsure as to how to address them with your mentor, you should feel free to seek the help and advice of the internship director. He or she can help you explore options for further improvement at your current job site and can discuss other options with you.

If you find that you don't like your internship at first, don't despair. Think about what is problematic and then work with your mentor and internship director to improve the situation.

Someone Else Is Constantly Taking Credit for My Work

LET'S SUPPOSE THAT YOU WORK at an advertising firm and your mentor has asked you to come up with some ideas for a new commercial. You do, and you present your ideas to your mentor for his consideration. Now let's suppose that he takes your ideas to the advertising director and she loves them! However, your mentor never mentions to her that the ideas were yours.

Why would this kind of situation occur at your internship? Of course, there will always be some people who will intentionally steal others' ideas or take credit for work they didn't do because they think it will be easier to "get ahead" if they

do. However, in most cases, mentors or supervisors may not even realize it if they pass your ideas off as their own. It may be that they don't actually realize the ideas or the work were yours to begin with; this is common in collaborative working environments in which people brainstorm and create things together. Or, it may be that some people don't realize that they *should* give you credit for your work, because you're "just an intern."

Whatever the reason, having someone else take credit for your work is frustrating. If you perceive that this is happening, we recom-

mend that you put your communication skills to work. Talk with the person whom you believe is "stealing your credit." Tell this person that you should receive credit for your ideas and your work and that it is unfair for him or her to pass off the work as his or her own. If this person doesn't realize what is happening, then this simple conversation may be all it takes to set the situation right. If the problem continues, we recommend that you consult your mentor about the appropriate way to address it.

People at Work Are Always Gossiping

THIS MAY BE A PROBLEM FOR **several** different reasons. Perhaps you are uncomfortable with gossip or find it to be unprofessional (it certainly can be). Perhaps the content of the gossip is of a nature that you find distasteful. Or, perhaps the problem is simply that the office gossip takes up time and interferes with your ability to complete your work in a timely and efficient manner.

If you have problems with gossip on a personal level, these are best addressed with people on a one-to-one basis. We don't recommend making a big deal out of it and coming across as if you are attempting to seize the moral high ground; that may alienate your coworkers and create tension for you on the job. However, you can politely deflect attempts to gossip with firm, but pleasant, explanations that you prefer to avoid it.

If your objection to gossip is that it is time-consuming or that people always want to gossip when you need to work, then the solution is also found in a direct, but pleasant, explanation. This time, you must explain that you have something to complete and cannot stop to chat. It's that simple. The problem with this solution is that it requires a good deal of firmness and resolution on your part as well as a good deal of tact. You don't want your gossiping coworker to leave with hurt feelings, so your tone is important. Make the explanation about your workload. You might offer to stop by his or her desk on your next break or, if you feel it is appropriate, ask if he or she wants to have lunch or coffee on a future date when work is not so pressing. If you make these offers or overtures, be sure to follow up.

Of course, you can use this approach to put off gossip that you simply find unappealing, and this method may avoid the problem of making you look like a spoilsport. However, if you simply defer gossip to another time when you are not so busy, you will remain in the gossip chain and will repeatedly have to address the issue of whether or not to engage in gossip. If your objection is really one of practice or content, it may be best to address that up front; it can save you some frustration and awkwardness later on.

I'm Not Being Taken Seriously at My Internship

THERE ARE MANY POSSIBLE reasons why people at your internship may not take you seriously. Some of them may be related to the attitudes of the people around you and the culture of the organization as a whole. However, before you determine that the problem is with your mentor or sponsoring organization, you should engage in some critical self-reflection and ask yourself whether you are contributing to the problem. As we have discussed in Chapters Three and Five, your appearance, demeanor, and understanding of your place within your organization can all affect how you are perceived. If you believe that you are not being taken seriously, then you should take a hard look at the way you dress (Are you complying with formal and informal expectations about professional dress within your organization?), your behavior (Are you on time for work and appointments? Are you perceived as confident and self-

assertive? Do you promote yourself as a valuable member of your team or department?), and your work product (Are you organized? Are you thoroughly prepared for meetings? Is your written work professionally presented and free from errors? Are you timely with your work?). These are things that can affect the way in which you are perceived on the job. A negative impression in any one of these areas can reduce your stature in the eyes of coworkers and supervisors and lead to changes in the way you are treated.

If you feel that you are doing all of these things to the best of your ability and that you are presenting a professional and competent image at work, then you may be facing biases or attitudes that are inherent to your workplace. These attitudes may be directed at your age, your perceived lack of work

experience, or—most unfortunately—your gender or your race. In these circumstances, the best general advice we can give you is to maintain your professional behavior and find ways to demonstrate your overall competence. This may mean going out of your way to request more responsibility and being prepared to argue that you are capable of handling such assignments if the initial response is to refuse to give them to you. Subtle forms of self-promotion can help you push your way into situations that will let you demonstrate the abilities that people may assume you do not have. If you feel that issues of age, gender, or race are seriously affecting the way in which you are being treated at work, then you should speak to your internship director about the situation.

Summary

IN THIS CHAPTER WE HAVE presented several different scenarios that are common for interns to encounter. Of course, you may face different challenges at your own internship. No matter what the situation, we encourage you to consult the internship director or coordinator if you are unsure as to how you should proceed.

Review Questions

1. Have you experienced any problems that you believe may be "common" but that Chapter Seven doesn't discuss? If so, describe the problem, how you've dealt with it, and whether you believe this strategy has been effective.

2. What are some general communication guidelines to keep in mind when talking to a mentor or peer about these challenges?

Chapter Eight

Dealing with Conflict

No MATTER WHAT KIND of work you do, one thing you will inevitably experience during your internship is conflict. Of course, we all have conflict from time to time; we experience it over a range of issues and in a number of relationships. We may deal with conflict well, or poorly, but we must all deal with it occasionally. In this chapter, we'll discuss what conflict is and what some of our options are for managing it. We'll also take a look at whether conflict is always a bad thing, or whether it might lead to some positive outcomes if managed properly.

What Is Conflict?

MANY OF US KNOW WHEN WE ARE experiencing conflict, but what is it that we're experiencing, exactly? In truth, conflict is a remarkably simple concept. It is exists whenever two or more people who have an interdependent relationship perceive that they have incompatible ideas, interests, or goals (see, e.g., Cahn, 1990; Canary, Cupach, & Messman, 1995; Cupach & Canary, 1997; Hocker & Wilmot, 1991). Several things about this definition are important to note. First, conflict requires the involvement of two or more people. Now, you might be saying, "Wait a minute; what about conflicts I have with myself?" It's true that we sometimes feel conflicted within ourselves. Let's say, for example, that you receive $100 as a birthday present from your grandparents—you might feel conflicted over whether to spend the money on something fun, like a new DVD player, or on something more sensible, like groceries or textbooks. This is certainly conflict, but it is intrapersonal (meaning "within the person"), and that's different from the type of conflict we'll be discussing in this chapter, which is more accurately thought of as interpersonal (meaning "between people").

A second important part of our definition is that the people involved must have an interdependent relationship. That is, they must have the type of relationship in which they influence and depend on each other. You might disagree with an opinion that is expressed in a letter to the editor in your local newspaper, but your disagreement doesn't necessarily constitute conflict, especially if you don't personally know the person who wrote the letter. The point here is that disagreement can only turn into conflict in relationships between people (or groups of people) who are interdependent. Think about the relationships in which you experience conflict most often. They might include your relationships with your parents, your roommates, your romantic partner, your siblings, your professors, or your boss or co-workers. Our relationships with these people are highly interdependent—that's part of what makes them important to us, but it's also part of what makes them prone to conflict.

Third, our definition requires that some incompatibility of ideas, interests, or goals be perceived. This tends to take one of two forms: Either the parties involved in the conflict are trying to accomplish different outcomes (e.g., you want to buy a swimming pool but your spouse wants to buy a hot tub) or else they are trying to accomplish the same goal through different means (e.g., you both want a pool, but you prefer to save the money to buy it, whereas your spouse prefers to borrow the money). In both cases, there is some incompatibility in what you're trying to do. Importantly, conflicts within our personal relationships range from trivial matters (e.g., what to prepare for dinner) to significant ones (e.g., whether or not to have children), and that's often true in our professional relationships, as well. A minor disagreement over when you'll take your lunch break at work is generally not as consequential as a major disagreement over

Conflict exists whenever two or more people who have an interdependent relationship perceive that they have incompatible ideas, interests, or goals.

company policy, yet both are examples of conflict.

When you think about conflict in this way, you probably realize that you experience it rather frequently. If so, you're not alone. As much as we may dislike conflict, it is a normal part of day-to-day social life for almost everyone. Given that, what should we do about it? It's nearly impossible to avoid, and as we'll discuss next, it does have some benefits as well as some drawbacks. Therefore, instead of focusing on how to prevent conflict, we'll direct our attention in his chapter on how best to manage it when we experience it. First, however, let's discuss what benefits conflict situation may offer us. Then, we'll address two aspects of conflict that matter to us in terms of how we might manage it: whether the conflict is real or merely perceived, and whether we are directly or indirectly involved.

Is Conflict Always a Bad Thing?

IT'S PRETTY EASY TO IDENTIFY THE negative things about conflict. Conflict can make us feel angry, or anxious, or stressed; it can damage our personal and professional relationships with people; and, it can even lead to health problems, such as hypertension, depression, or premature aging. Does that mean that conflict is always bad?

Actually, it might surprise you to learn that conflict can actually be good for individuals and their relationships. The key seems to be not in the amount of conflict that is experienced but in how it is managed. You can probably think of a time when you have gotten into an argument with someone, only to find later that, as a result of your argument, you developed a new idea or a new way of thinking about something. Conflict, in and of itself, can help us do that, because it highlights differences in our perspectives and allows (or forces!) us to consider points of view that are at odds with our own. In doing so, we are often exposed to ideas that hadn't occurred to us before but which may be worth considering. That doesn't mean we always enjoy the process of managing conflict, but if we manage it well, we may find that the outcomes actually strengthen our relationships with other people. Therefore, the conflicts that emerge in the course of your internship can actually bring about helpful learning experiences, even strengthening your professional ties and deepening your understanding of workplace relationships—but only if conflicts are well-managed.

Real v. Merely Perceived Conflict

WE MENTIONED ABOVE THAT conflict involves a perceived incompatibility in ideas, interests, or goals. The adjective *perceived* is important here because it recognizes that conflict can arise even in cases when ideas, interests, or goals are actually compatible, although we perceive them not to be. We call this type of situation a misunderstanding, and you have probably experienced this many times before.

Let's say, for example, that Andy and his wife, Maureen, have decided to buy a new vehicle. Andy believes that they ought to buy a truck, whereas Maureen favors buying an SUV. The two express their disagreement on the topic; Andy points out all of the advantages of having a truck while Maureen suggests that an SUV is much more practical. This is clearly an example of conflict. However, when the two go to the dealership to actually make their purchase, it turns out that they both want the same vehicle—although Andy had been calling it a truck and Maureen had been calling it an SUV, they both had the same vehicle in mind the whole time. Thus, although they were having conflict, their conflict was not genuine, because their goals were actually the same. Rather, their conflict was merely perceived: Even though their goals were identical, they perceived them to be different, and their conflict rested on this presumption of difference. Once they cleared up their misunderstanding, however, they discovered that they had both wanted the same thing all along.

When experiencing conflict, it can be extremely helpful to keep in mind that the difference in ideas, interests, or goals may be genuine or it may not. In the latter case, resolving the conflict can be as simple a matter as being explicit about what each person is striving for and comparing them to discover whether they really are at odds or not.

Direct v. Indirect Involvement in Conflict

ANOTHER ASPECT OF CONFLICT that can have implications for how you should manage it is whether you are directly or indirectly involved. In general, we are directly involved in a conflict when we are one of the interdependent parties with incompatible ideas, interests, or goals. If you have an argument with your professor over what grade you deserve in a class, then you are directly involved in that conflict. However, we can also be involved in conflict indirectly. This happens when we are not one of the parties in a conflict but we have a personal or professional interest in how it gets resolved. Perhaps it is your best friend, rather than you, who is contesting his or her grade. In this case, your friend and the professor are the parties in the conflict, so you are not directly involved. You support your friend and believe he or she deserves a better grade, but the conflict does involve you indirectly. Even though it isn't your own grade on the line, you have an interest in seeing that your friend is treated fairly, and so you have an indirect involvement in the conflict.

This, too, is a common situation, and it calls for a certain amount of tact to handle it well. Sometimes, as in the case of your friend's conflict with a professor, it is clear where your loyalties lie: You support your friend because he or she is your friend. However, you may be taking the class, too, which means that attitudes and behaviors also affect you. In this type of situation, we are called upon to give support to the "side" we agree with while also watching out for our own interests. (In the course of supporting your friend, you probably wouldn't want to make your professor angry at you.)

In other cases, you might find that your loyalties lie equally on both sides of the issue. You can probably think of times when people you care about have been in conflict with each other and you have felt "put in the middle." Perhaps you are friends with two of your co-workers, but they dislike each other. When they're in conflict, then, you may feel torn between them. In such cases, handling the situation tactfully is even more important. Even though you are only indirectly involved in the conflict, you still have the goal of maintaining your relationships with each of your co-workers.

Whenever you are indirectly involved in a conflict, it's in your best interests to consider carefully how to handle the situation. Just because a conflict doesn't affect you directly, it may affect you indirectly in any number of ways, and it's important to keep that in mind when deciding whether to get involved in the situation.

When you are involved in conflict, either directly or indirectly, you have several options for how to manage it. Below, we'll discuss the three more common strategies that people use for dealing with conflict situations. None of these is going to be appropriate for every circumstance; you must use what you know about communication to ascertain each situation and determine how best to proceed.

Strategies for Managing Conflict

EVERY CONFLICT SITUATION IS unique, and how we choose to manage conflict will depend somewhat on the specifics of the situation, whether the conflict is real or merely perceived, and whether we are directly or indirectly involved. In general, however, researchers have discovered that we tend to take one of three distinct approaches to managing conflict when we experience it.

One approach is known as a distributive strategy. In this approach, we focus on the competition between people (and specifically between their incompatible ideas, interests, and goals), so that the moti-

vation is for one of the parties in the conflict to prevail and for the other to lose. Let's say that you and your boss are having a conflict over your salary: you insist that you need and deserve a raise but your boss refuses. Taking a distributive approach to this conflict would mean that you focus your energies on what it would take to convince your boss to give you the raise, while your boss holds his or her ground and continues to insist that you cannot or should not receive one. In other words, both of you are working to "win" the conflict, which would mean in this case

Conflict is not always bad for relationships. Many quality relationships are characterized by high degrees of conflict. What often matters is not how much conflict a relationship has, but how the conflict is managed.

that the other person "loses." Confrontation, persistent arguing, negative affect, and back-and-forth discussion are among the behaviors that are commonly observed when people use a distributive strategy for managing their conflict.

A second approach, appropriately named an avoidant strategy, involves managing the conflict by ignoring or minimizing it. If you were to take an avoidant approach to managing a conflict with your boss over a raise, you might avoid talking about the issue with him or her but instead try to convince your coworkers that you deserve a raise, hoping they will indirectly put pressure on your boss to agree. Or, you might instead just avoid the topic altogether, and quietly resent your boss instead of resolving your differences of opinion. Obviously, strategies of this nature aren't very productive because they ultimately leave the conflict unresolved. However, as you might guess, avoidance is actually a fairly common way for people to manage conflict. People often decide that it is easier just to live with conflict than to take the steps necessary to resolve it, and the reason for this should be clear: Conflict isn't fun. Most of us don't like it, and some people find it to be extremely uncomfortable. Avoidance, then, can sometimes seem like the lesser of two evils.

Finally, we can take what is known as an integrative strategy. In this approach, we work with the other party to compromise and try to reach a solution to the conflict that is acceptable to both parties. If you were to take an integrative approach to your salary conflict, you and your boss might agree that, instead of receiving a raise right now, you would receive an increase in your vacation time and then receive a raise in six months, when you have more seniority. Unlike the distributive approach, which creates a "win-lose" situation, the integrative approach strives for a "win-win" situation. With an integrative approach, neither party gets exactly what it wants, but both parties get something they can live with.

The integrative strategy probably strikes you as the most desirable approach to managing conflict, and in many cases, it is. It should be noted, though, that there are times when the other strategies may be more appropriate. When parents have conflict with their children, for instance, compromise is not always called for; it may be more appropriate for the parents' will to prevail. And, in situations when addressing conflict directly might lead to destructive behaviors (such as physical violence), avoidance might actually be the best alternative. It should be clear to you by now that no single approach to managing conflict will work in every situation. By learning what the various alternatives are, however, you equip yourself to deal with a variety of conflict situations that you might face.

Summary

IN ONE FORM OR ANOTHER, conflict is an inevitable part of our interactions with other people. In this chapter, we've discussed several aspects of conflict, including what it is, what options we have for managing it, and why conflict can sometimes lead to positive results. As you review this material, keep in mind that every relationship is different, and thus, the strategies you use to manage conflict in those relationships may also differ. We hope that the information we've discussed here will help you to deal with those situations.

Review Questions

1. What is conflict? Is every disagreement a conflict?

2. What things should be considered when deciding how to respond to conflict?

3. Is there one way of managing conflict that works best in all situations, or are there situations in which each form of conflict management is appropriate?

4. Analyze a conflict that has emerged during your internship. What strategies did the parties to the conflict use to manage it? Do you believe the conflict was well managed? Why or why not?

For Further Reading

Cahn, D. D. (Ed.) (1990). *Intimates in conflict: A communication perspective*. Hillsdale, NJ: Erlbaum.

Canary, D. J., Cupach, W. R., & Messman, S. J. (1995). *Relationship conflict: Conflict in parent-child, friendship, and romantic relationships*. Thousand Oaks, CA: Sage.

Hocker, J. L., & Wilmot, W. W. (1991). *Interpersonal conflict* (3rd ed.). Dubuque, IA: Brown.

Chapter Nine

Your Communication Education

I F YOU ARE CLOSE TO finishing your college education, you are probably focused on the future, and rightly so. However, as we'll discuss in more detail in Chapter Ten, part of your future success will depend on your ability to apply what you've learned over the last several years. Suppose you're in a job interview and your prospective employer says, "Tell me about being a communication major; what does that mean?" You will want to answer in a way that demonstrates at least a basic understanding of the communication discipline and some of the major ideas you have studied. In this short chapter, we provide you with a brief overview of how the communication discipline has evolved and what it currently entails, and of how people in the discipline use theories and ideas to inform their work.

The Communication Discipline

MANY UNIVERSITIES AROUND the country have communication departments, although they may be called communication arts, communication studies, speech communication, human communication, or even theater arts. Most such departments offer the baccalaureate degree in communication, and many also offer the masters and doctorate degrees. Compared to many other areas of study, such as political science, chemistry, or music, communication is relatively young. The communication discipline evolved primarily from English and literature studies; early communication departments focused their courses on rhetoric and analysis of texts, which is similar to what is taught in many English departments today. Later, social scientists migrated from disciplines such as psychology and sociology and began applying their methods to the study of communication behaviors between people; those interested in media and mass communication began to apply their areas of focus; and some from theater and performance studies departments joined the communication discipline to focus on the performance of literature and other texts. Over time, a complete academic discipline has evolved.

Today, the communication discipline is growing and flourishing.

There are several professional associations that allow professors and students from across the country to meet and share their research ideas. The two largest organizations are the National Communication Association (NCA) and the International Communication Association (ICA). Despite what their names might suggest, NCA is the larger and more powerful of the two organizations. It holds its annual conventions in November of each year, while ICA meets annually sometime between May and July. At these conventions, communication professors and students come together to discuss current research and teaching principles, adopt policies related to the discipline, and learn about new developments in higher education. There are also regional associations for each of the four major U.S. regions (Western, Southern, Central, and Eastern) that meet each spring. And people in specific areas of the discipline often belong to other organizations that address their particular interests, such as the Association of Educators in Journalism and Mass Communication (AEJMC) or the International Association for Relationship Research (IARR).

While all of these organizations listed above are great resources for undergraduates with interests in academic research careers, other national organizations also exist that are designed to aid your professional development outside of academia. Organizations such as the International Association for Business Communicators (IABC) and the Public Relations Student Society of America may have local chapters on your campus. These may or may not be housed in your communication department. Additionally, your department may have a communication honors society or communication student association. Getting involved in these organizations (even if you are about to graduate) will give you opportunities to meet and network with active professionals that have well-developed careers in communication.

The communication discipline is among the most diverse fields in the social and behavioral sciences.

How would you describe your communication education to a prospective employer?

During your college education you have probably been exposed to several of the specific content areas that the discipline includes. Here we will introduce you to some of these content areas, which are taught in communication departments around the country.

Instructional communication looks at communication in educational settings, including interaction involving students, teachers, parents, and school administrators. *Intercultural communication* focuses on how people from diverse cultural, ethnic, social, economic, and religious backgrounds communicate and understand each other. *Interpersonal communication* deals with communication in relationships, including friendships, romantic relationships, families, work relationships, and even among strangers. *Intrapersonal communication* looks at how we "communicate" with ourselves by engaging in thoughts and self-talk. *Mass communication* focuses on the use of radio, television, print media, the internet, and other media as channels for communicating to a broad audience. *Organizational communication* is the study of interaction in organizations, whether they are formal (like a company or university) or informal (like a neighborhood or social group). *Performance studies* deals with the public performance of various texts, such as literature, and with the per-

formative aspects of human communication as a whole. *Political communication* looks at how communication is used in legislative, judicial, and other political contexts and how it is used to shape public opinion and policy. *Rhetoric* is the study of texts, persuasion, and argumentation; rhetoricians often analyze historic or contemporary texts to understand how arguments are constructed and points are made. *Small group communication* is the study of interaction and decision-making in small groups, such as committees, clubs, and families.

These are some of the major areas of emphasis within the discipline. There are several others that are more focused in their orientation, such as health communication, family communication, First Amendment/freedom of speech studies, ethnography, advertising, and the like. With so many areas of study, the communication discipline truly offers something for almost everyone.

So why are we telling you about all of these different areas of the communication discipline? We've provided this description because many people outside of academia may have misconceptions about what you've been studying. For instance, when many people (e.g., job interviewers) hear that you

have a degree in communication, they may assume that you've been studying broadcasting, which is a serious misunderstanding of the skills and knowledge base you've developed if you are not a mass communication major. As you enter the job market, you will need to have a plan for how you will explain what you've been learning for the last few years and how these skills relate to the workplace.

The good news is that as our economy becomes increasingly information- and service-based, the skill set a communication major can offer is quite attractive to prospective employers—if you make an effort to effectively explain the content of your major. Moreover, the discipline of communication has always been interested in the development of broad-based skills that can be used to address a variety of practical problems (e.g., public speaking, conflict management, critical thinking, persuading others, communication in teams and groups, management communication). Thus, your major offers the broad background of a liberal arts degree that will allow you to move in a variety of career directions. However, in addition to this versatility, you have developed specific skills that will be useful in a variety of contexts, unlike some liberal arts majors.

Communication Theories

IF YOU'RE LIKE MANY undergraduates, you have come across several different communication theories in your coursework. However, you may be left wondering things like "What are theories, exactly?" or "What difference do they make to me?" Entire volumes have been written on these topics; here, we'll offer some answers to these questions in a more condensed form.

In principle, a theory is just an explanation for something. At times, you have probably noticed something happening around you and said, "I have a theory about that." What you meant is that you have an explanation, or a way of understanding why something happened. Let's say that one of your best friends ignored you when you passed by her on campus this

morning. Could you come up with a theory for that? One theory might be that she was so preoccupied that she didn't even notice you were there. A different theory could be that she was angry with you for some reason, or that she was so behind schedule that she didn't have time to talk. Each of these provides a completely different explanation for the same event, giving you several theories to work with.

The theories used by researchers are more detailed, of course, but they operate in much the same way, each providing some type of answer to the "why" question. Why do friends sometimes ignore you? Why do we form friendships in the first place? Why do we care about some friends more than others? Communication researchers have theories about these and a whole host of other issues.

Before we discuss communication theories in particular, we want you to know a couple of things about theories in general. First, *a theory is always a theory.* You have probably heard people say that some theories, like the theory of relativity or the theory of evolution, are so commonly accepted that they are now regarded as fact. This type of statement reflects a misunderstanding about the nature of theory. Here's what we want you to know: a theory is an idea, and it always remains an idea. Scientists never prove theories to be right or wrong; they can't, because a theory is just an idea. You'll understand what we mean in a moment.

If theories can never be proven, then what good are they? Well, when we have a good theory about <u>why</u> something happens, we can use it to make predictions about <u>when</u> and <u>how</u> it will happen. These predictions <u>can</u> be tested and proven right or wrong. If they're proven right, then they give support to the theory, but the theory itself is never directly tested. To use an example, let's suppose we came up with theories about why the sun always rises in the East and sets in the West. Your theory (which we'll call Theory X) is that the sun isn't "rising" at all; rather, the earth is rotating in a certain direction, which causes us to perceive that the sun rises and sets. The direction of the earth's rotation makes it appear that the sun rises in the East and sets in the West. My theory (which we'll call Theory Y) is that a great cosmic wind, blowing in outer space, pushes the sun around the Earth in a westward direction, and if that wind ever changes direction, the sun could rise in the North and set in the South.

Which theory is right? We don't really know! Yes, Theory Y sounds pretty far-fetched, but keep in mind that, until just a few hundred years ago, the best scientists in the world thought that the earth was flat and that it was the center of the entire universe. There are probably things that we are "certain" of today that will sound ridiculous to people in another few hundred years. The point here is that people will always have different theories for the same things, and it doesn't really matter if a theory is right or wrong because we can never prove it to be right or wrong. It will always be one explanation among many.

However, our second point is that *theories lead to predictions that can be tested.* These predictions are called hypotheses. Notice that both Theory X and Theory Y pre-

---

Figure 9.1

Explanation and Prediction

A good theory *explains* things and helps us to *predict* things. But how are explanation and prediction related? If we have one of these abilities, do we always have the other?

- *If we can explain, can we always predict?* Suppose you understand why it rains; you know all the conditions that lead to rain and how they work together. Does this give you the ability to predict when it will rain?

- *If we can predict, can we always explain?* Let's say that your neighbor turns on her porch light every time it snows. You have witnessed this time and time again, so you can predict that when it snows again, that light will come on. Does this give you the ability to explain why?

dict that the sun rises in the East (at least for now). This hypothesis can be tested—we can watch the sun every day to see from which direction it rises—and it can be proven to be either true or false. When hypotheses are shown to be true, they lend support to the theories they came from, but they don't prove that the explanation is true, just that the prediction is true. Keep in mind that if our hypothesis about the sun is proven, it supports *both* Theory X *and* Theory Y!

Of course, there is more evidence overall to support Theory X than Theory Y, and so we would say that Theory X is the better or more useful of the two theories...not that it is true, just that it is better. Again, it's just an explanation, and we can come up with other theories that explain and predict the same thing. After all, we quickly came up with several theories about why your friend ignored you, but they all explained the same event.

Communication researchers use a number of theories to explain and predict why people communicate they way they do. Some theories are unique to the communication

discipline, and others are theories that have developed in other areas of study. Researchers in interpersonal communication, for instance, have several theories about how people form relationships, such as uncertainty reduction theory (Berger & Calabrese, 1975), social penetration theory (Altman & Taylor, 1973), attraction theory (Byrne, 1971), or attachment theory (Bartholomew & Horowitz, 1991). There are theories about why people lie (e.g., information manipulation theory; McCornack, 1992); why people can be scared into changing their behaviors (e.g., extended parallel process model; Witte, 1992); how people explain other people's behaviors (e.g., attribution theory; Heider, 1959); why people express affection to others (e.g., affection exchange theory; Floyd, 2001); or how people respond to unexpected events (e.g., expectancy violations theory; Burgoon & Hale, 1988).

Often, different theories will explain the same event differently. Why do you become friends with certain people and not with others, for example? Uncertainty reduction theory would say that you are more

likely to become friends with people if you can reduce your level of uncertainty about them. Attraction theory would say that you are more likely to become friends with people who are similar to you. Attachment theory would say that you have a general pattern of how you make friends that was formed during the first days of your life. Each of these theories explains the same event (you making friends) but in a completely different way. Moreover, each theory causes us to look at different variables in the situation, like your level of uncertainty, your perceived similarity, or your attachment style. Depending on which theory they use, then, communication researchers measure different things and test their predictions differently.

Our examples here have come mostly from interpersonal communication, but researchers in all areas of the communication discipline use theories to help them understand what they study. You have probably been exposed to the major theories in your particular area of interest as you have taken your communication coursework.

Summary

TO BE SURE, THESE SUMMARIES of the nature of the discipline and the nature and uses of theory are very abbreviated, and to some degree, they reflect our particular way of thinking. Other communication researchers would probably have written these sections a little differently. However, we hope they have provided you with at least a cursory review of some of the things you should know about your communication education. This review will be helpful to you as you complete your internship course and, we hope, as you prepare for the working world. We will address the latter issue in greater detail in the next chapter.

Review Questions

1. What are the most important things I've learned as a communication major?

2. If someone asks you what it means to be a communication major, what do you believe is the best way to explain it?

3. How does a theory work? What theories have I studied during my education?

4. Pick a communication theory you have studied in your coursework and apply it to a situation you have experienced or observed in your internship. What does that theory explain about the communication you experienced or observed?

For Further Reading

Littlejohn, S. W. (1996). *Theories of human communication* (5th ed.). Belmont, CA: Wadsworth.

Chapter Ten

After the Internship

BECAUSE YOU ARE DOING your internship toward the end of your undergraduate career, you will probably be looking for full-time employment very soon. You may have gone through an application and interview process to obtain your internship, or you may have other experience in job hunting. Regardless of how experienced or inexperienced you are, looking for a job can be a stressful and overwhelming process. This chapter will provide some general advice on preparing for and executing your job search and some more specific advice on resumes, cover letters, and interviews.

Starting Out: What to Know and What to Expect

IF THERE ARE TWO BASIC principles that you should embrace as you begin to search for a job, they are: 1) *know yourself*, and 2) *know your major*. Before you do anything else, you need to think about who you are and how you want to begin your career. This means taking an inventory of the things that are important to you in a job. Do you work best alone? Do you prefer autonomy, or do you need structure? Are you creative? Do you love dealing with the public or hate the thought of it? What sort of hours do you expect to work? How much travel are you willing to do? Each of these may seem like an easy question, but taken together the answers will tell you a lot about the kind of position and the kind of employer you ought to be looking for.

In addition to knowing yourself, take some time to think about your major and what you learned in college. This doesn't mean simply typing a list of the courses you took. Rather, it means understanding what it is that we do in the communication field and why what we do is important. A degree in communication may not strike a business manager, an accountant, or a project engineer as being relevant to what they do. Most everyone knows what an accounting major does, but not everyone will know what a communication major does. You will have to be able to "sell" your degree when you interview for a job; that means making your prospective employer understand how your skills and knowledge about communication are valuable. Refer back to Chapter Nine for a review of major communication principles and processes.

As you go through this initial process, it is also important that you set realistic goals and expectations. While you should not be afraid to apply for positions that may stretch your existing skills and abilities to a degree, don't expect to be able to skip significant steps along the path of your career development. Being realistic also applies to expectations about potential salaries, benefits, and certain lifestyle considerations. After all, entry-level management trainees aren't usually handed keys to the executive washroom! Most of us must expect to do a fair amount of "grunt" work until we have worked our way into a higher-level position.

Researching the job market in the city and profession that interests you can help you determine what some reasonable expectations might be. Of course, when you compare salaries between companies, be sure that the positions and the other job conditions are actually comparable. Does the entry-level position at Company X pay significantly more than the one at Company Y because it requires extensive travel or unusually large time commitments at night and on weekends? You can do this research through newspaper advertisements, online job placement services, and through the Web sites made available by organizations, many of which include information about employment opportunities. The career placement office (sometimes called a placement center or a career center) on your campus may also be a great source of information on these issues.

Before you begin your job search, it's important that you spend some time thinking about how to describe yourself and how to describe your communication education to a prospective employer.

Starting Early and Searching Effectively

ONE IMPORTANT THING TO remember about job searching is that it can take time. Not only does it take time to do the research you need to do in order to search effectively, it also takes time to prepare your resume, write your cover letters, and to otherwise work your way through the interview process. We suggest that you treat your job search as though it is one of your classes; you should dedicate as much time every week to your job search as you ideally would to one of your classes. One of the first things you should do is begin to work on your resume and have it ready when opportunities arise. You will also want to line up potential references and ask for letters of recommendation in advance. People are more receptive to helping you with these things if you give them advance notice and permit them to help you in ways that are convenient for them.

Keep in mind, too, that jobs become available at a variety of times, and if you wait until the day after graduation to start looking, you may discover that a number of good positions were filled in March. Some students think they can't look for work until after graduation because they won't be available until then. However, many employers will adjust their starting dates to accommodate you. The point is that you never know until you try. When we talk about cover letters later in this chapter, we will mention ways that you can prevent confusion and frustration on your part or on the part of potential employers by addressing your anticipated start date up front.

Starting early also gives you the best chance at developing more than one option for yourself. If you aren't sure whether you want to go into marketing or advertising, you can take your time and interview with a variety of companies. If you wait until you graduate, you may feel pressure to take the first job that comes along, even if you aren't sure it's a good fit for you.

How you search is just as important as when you search. Many universities have career placement offices that will sponsor career fairs and provide other job-search services. Whatever the reputation of your career services office is, you owe it to yourself to check out its resources and make use of whatever you can. Again, the key is

quired to post your resume online, be sure you do so in an internet-friendly format that will look professional after it's posted. If you have to retype your resume or type other statements for posting, then be sure you proofread for errors. While we may be used to the informality of e-mail and online chat, don't let the familiarity of the computer lull you into being casual with these postings and interactions.

You might also consider doing some informational interviewing to aid you in your job search. In

> *How you search is just as important as when you search. Many universities have career placement offices that will sponsor career fairs and provide other job-search services. Whatever the reputation of your career services office is, you owe it to yourself to check out its resources and make use of whatever you can.*

planning in advance. Showing up at career services the month before graduation and expecting to find a job waiting for you is unreasonable. Make an effort to find out what services are offered, when they recommend you start looking, what types of employers they work with, and when their job fairs will be held.

In addition to using career services, you can take advantage of online job placement services. These vary in the types of jobs they advertise, so you will have to look around and find one that fits your needs. Take this avenue of job searching as seriously as you would any other interaction with a potential employer. If you are re-

the context of a job search, an informational interview is one in which you simply meet with a professional who works in an occupation that interests you in order to develop a realistic picture of what the work is actually like, what skills and qualifications are necessary, and how a typical career path in an occupation evolves. This person may even allow you to "shadow" them for a day. You might make contact with this person through your internship, a professor, a family member or family friend, a student organization on campus or through a local professional organization. Because you are not actually interviewing for a job, these exchanges can be very informative. Some students assume that working professionals are reluctant to participate in these sessions, but you might be surprised by how much people like to talk about themselves and their experiences. You might also be pleasantly surprised (and lucky!) if the person interviewing you happens to know of a job available in their industry and volunteers to serve as a reference.

It may seem like a good idea to make your search as broad as possible, but you should keep in mind that following up on possible interviews and requests for information is a time-consuming process for you and for potential employers. So, be reasonable in the way in which you construct your online search. And, with regard to following up, be sure to check your e-mail, your job search accounts or mailboxes, and any

other points of contact that potential employers might use. After all, you don't want to make it hard for a potential employer to get in touch with you; if a company you are interested in sends you an e-mail asking for more information or offering you an interview, you don't want to wait three weeks to respond!

Your Resume

PREPARING YOUR RESUME IS one of the first things you need to consider when you begin to job search. Your resume is your ticket into an interview. That's why it is important to put some thought and effort into constructing a resume that represents you in the best ways possible. Everyone has different skills, experiences, and strong points, so no two resumes will be identical. But there are some general suggestions that we can recommend as you prepare yours.

First, keep the length of your resume to one page. In some professions (such as higher education), resumes may be expected to go beyond one page, but for most fields this is not the case. Remember, your resume is not an autobiography. It is simply a way of introducing your most marketable qualities to the world. Once you get the interview you can fill in the details and elaborate on points of particular interest. In order to get the interview, keep your resume brief, clear, and professional.

As a full-time student, you should highlight your education by putting it first on your resume. We discussed in the previous chapter that you may need to make an extra effort to explain your communication major.

Many people who look at your resume may not understand specifically what a communication major has been studying, so you will want to go beyond merely listing your major as "communication." Fortunately, there are a few relatively simple ways to do this. Since most universities and departments require communication majors to declare a specific interest area or areas, it may be helpful to list this on your resume. For example, it might mean having an additional line that that states "Emphasis: Organizational Communication" or "Emphases: Advertising and Public Relations." Another way to emphasize the value of your major is to list areas of coursework that are particularly relevant to the jobs you are applying for. Use terms that resume readers are likely to understand while still being honest about what you have studied. For example, in addition to having a line on your resume that lists your major, you may also wish to have a line that states, "Advanced coursework: interpersonal communication, communication in teams and groups, and management communication." Finally, if you have enough available space, you may wish to list a couple of major projects you completed that might be of interest to

employers, such as group presentations or organizational case studies.

In addition to your education, highlight any work experiences you have had that demonstrate skills, abilities, or knowledge that will be relevant to the positions for which you are applying. When listing these work experiences, the content and formatting should emphasize the *job* you did (e.g., marketing associate), not the employer you worked for. And don't forget to list your internship!

Take the time to write effective descriptions of your previous work experience. As a communication major, you should know that word choice matters, yet many people make the mistake of choosing pas-

Remember that your resume is not an autobiography. Its purpose is not to tell your life story—rather, its purpose is to get you an interview.

sive language that does not persuasively illustrate to prospective employers what you actually *did* in a particular job. Be sure to use active verbs and specific, descriptive phrases in these job descriptions. For example, if you were a customer service supervisor, it would be far more effective to say that you "maintained customer satisfaction by coordinating merchandise exchanges and returns, resolving conflicts with clients, and designing and implementing a new quality control system" than simply stating "exchanged merchandise, took customer complaints, and worked with quality control." The more action-oriented and explanatory description communicates your responsibilities and accomplishments more effectively because it portrays them in a more universal manner. You may not be applying for a customer service job, but your ability to keep clients satisfied, experience with conflict resolution, and initiative in developing a new system will likely be attractive to a variety of prospective employers, whether or not their jobs involve customer service.

You should also include your school activities, leadership positions held, community service or volunteer work done, or special awards and honors you have received. These items can help demonstrate qualities and characteristics such as leadership, dedication, determination, reliability, or maturity that may not come across in other ways.

While you work on the content of your resume, keep in mind that appearance counts. Spend time considering the layout and format. We recommend, unless you are looking for work as a graphic artist, that you avoid using fancy fonts, unusual colors, and nontraditional formats. You want to be remembered for your outstanding skills and qualifications, not for the color or typestyle of your resume. Besides being distracting, fancy fonts and unusual design elements can cause problems if your resume has to be faxed, scanned, or e-mailed. Many books and Web sites have specific suggestions for preparing resumes just for electronic transmission, but just keeping your resume simple and clean can help avoid many potential problems. On the other hand, you don't want your resume to lack any formatting at all; this might make it difficult to read and could suggest a lack of effort on your part.

Finally—and this point will be made again when we get to cover letters—we cannot stress enough how important it is to proofread your resume very carefully. You should proofread it yourself, obviously, but you should also have someone reliable and detail-oriented proofread it for you. If there is ever a time to shoot for perfection, this is it. Remember that your resume is the first impression that many potential employers will have of you. You need for this impression to be professional in every way. The extra effort you put into this portion of your job search will be worth it in the long run.

For your help, we have included sample resumes in Appendix E. Importantly, these are only examples; they do not represent the only way, or necessarily even the best way, to put a resume together, but they can give you some ideas. Of course, you will want to write your resume to fit your particular qualifications and the specific type of job you are seeking.

Your References

MANY EMPLOYERS WILL ASK YOU to provide references during the interview process. To save room on your resume, you can prepare your list of references on a separate piece of paper. It's also a good idea to indicate whether each reference is a personal or professional reference, and you should have at least one of each. Personal references will be able to tell potential employers about your personality and what you are like to be around. Profes-

sional references can provide information about your work ethic, abilities, and what you are like on the job. Of course, you do not want to list someone as a reference without first checking with him or her. This way, when your potential employer calls to ask about you, your reference will be prepared to present you in the best light possible.

Some employers may ask for letters of recommendation instead of

a list of references. Letters of recommendation should be as specific as possible about what you have to offer a potential employer. Broad, glowing statements that are not grounded in specific instances or examples are unlikely to be persuasive. Since you have to expect that people will be honest in these letters, you need to be careful about whom you ask for a letter of recommendation; you should be sure that the person you are asking is comfortable giving you a positive reference. As uncomfortable as this may appear to be, it is better to find out up front that the reference may not be all you would like. Of course, you should also consider the credibility of each reference. All other things being equal, you want to obtain recommendations from people who will command respect by virtue of their professional experiences or reputations.

Figure 10.1

Frequently Asked Questions about Resumes and Interviews

Q: Should I list my grade point average on my resume?

A: Advice on this issue varies. If your GPA is outstanding (say, over a 3.7 on a 4.0 scale), then putting it on your resume shouldn't hurt you. If it is less than exceptional then leaving it off may avoid calling attention to it and permit you to form a first impression on the basis of other things. Of course, if a potential employer assumes that you've left your GPA off of your resume because it is lower than desired, she may ask you about it. Be prepared to address this issue should it come up.

Q: Do I need to use expensive paper for my resume?

A: Not necessarily. While we don't recommend using copier paper, it is not necessary to spend a lot of money on paper. Where you should spend your money is on the printing and/or photocopying used to produce your resume. If you are sending out a large number of resumes, you may choose to laser print an original and then photocopy the others; it is fine to do this, but it is best to have a professional copy center make the copies for you in order to obtain the best clarity possible.

Q: Should I use colored paper, colored ink, or unusual layouts in order to make my resume more memorable?

A: Unless you are applying for a position in the graphic arts, we advise you to keep your resume very traditional. Use white or off-white paper. Use black ink. As we discuss in this chapter, you want to be remembered for your skills and not for your unusual design choices.

Q: Should I fax or e-mail my resume to a potential employer?

A: That depends on the organization and what it wants. Many job advertisements or postings will specify a contact person and a way to make contact; in these cases, you will obviously want to abide by their wishes. If there is no preference stated, look at the contact information provided. If they list a fax number as well as an address, then you might consider sending your resume by both methods. In these cases, make sure that your cover letter clearly explains the purpose of your communication.

Figure 10.1 continued

Q: Should I call to follow up after I send my resume?

A: Many job postings will specify "no phone calls." So, in those cases the answer is easy: As hard as it is to wait, you must abide by the wishes of the organization. If there is no such specification, then you may consider calling or e-mailing to follow up. However, once is enough; you should refrain from calling back or e-mailing repeatedly. The last thing you want to do is make a pest of yourself. Hopefully, potential employers will respond to inquiries promptly and will let you know when your materials have been received and/or when a decision has been made, but they may not provide this information as fast as you would like. The best thing you can do is to be patient!

Q: Should I list basic computer skills on my resume?

A: Not if they are basic. In today's world, everyone expects a college graduate to be able to use basic word processing programs and have some familiarity with the Internet. Even basic desktop publishing, spreadsheet, and database skills are not that unusual for educated people to have. If you achieved certification in a particular programming language or have extensive expertise in a particular area like Web design or graphic arts, you should consider adding these skills to your resume if you have room and if they are relevant to the type of work you are seeking.

Q: Should I list all of my clubs and activities on my resume?

A: These things can help you demonstrate leadership, time management, and interpersonal skills that don't necessarily get reflected in your work experience or grades. For that reason, it is useful to include activities on your resume. However, keep in mind that space is limited. If you have a large number of activities that you have participated in, choose the ones that best reflect the type of skills and experiences that you want to promote with potential employers. Also, keep in mind that if you list a membership or activity on your resume, you are opening the door for discussion of these topics. As we explain elsewhere in this chapter, certain topics, such as religion, are off-limits during the interview. If you include these items on your resume, you make it possible for the interviewer to ask you about them.

Q: I'm really nervous about the interviewing process. What can I do?

A: If your anxiety is situational (that is, it is primarily due to the stress associated with the interview process), you can try to relieve it through some of the same techniques used to fight anxiety associated with public speaking. Deep breathing exercises and visualizing positive outcomes, while they may feel silly at first, can help relieve the build up of nervous tension prior to an interview. Another thing that helps is practice. Think about common or likely interview questions and practice your answers out loud. In addition, doing adequate research about the company and job position prior to the interview can give you the self-assurance you need to approach the situation calmly. A final helpful thing to keep in mind is that the interview is as much an opportunity for you to interview the company as it is for the company to interview you. If you think of the interview as a two-way exchange of information, ideas, and values, it may relieve some of the pressure you feel going into the situation.

Your Cover Letter

IF YOUR RESUME IS YOUR TICKET to an interview, then your cover letter is what gets your resume read in the first place. Your cover letter should be tailored to the particular position you are applying for. This includes using the name of the person doing the hiring and how the name is spelled. Of course, if you go to the trouble of finding out that Kory Floyd is doing the hiring, don't blow your good first impression by sending the letter to Cory Floyd! Remember that even common names like John or Judy can be spelled in more than one way.

Your cover letter should not try to restate everything that is on your resume. This is merely an introduction—like a good lead to a news story, it whets the appetite of the people reading it and makes them want to know more about you. Your cover letter should highlight the most important qualifications or experiences you bring to the job and should refer the reader to your resume for additional information. Aesthetically, your cover letter should match your resume in paper type, color, font style, and layout. That conveys a very professional image to the person receiving your materials. Again, your cover letter should be perfect. Have it proofread for grammatical errors, spelling errors, spacing errors, and overall clarity.

We have included two sample cover letters in Appendix F. Again, these are only examples; you will want to craft your cover letter so that it highlights your specific qualifications.

Your Interview

IF YOUR EFFORTS UP TO THIS point have paid off by getting you an interview, congratulations. Now is your chance to shine. The job interview is likely to be your first opportunity to make a face-to-face impression on potential employers. As you may know from your communication courses, the primacy effect makes first impressions very important. A good first impression can withstand many negative experiences in the future, but a poor first impression will outlast a large number of future positive experiences.

The impression you make in the interview will depend a great deal on how you look. You should be sure to dress in appropriate professional attire. What is appropriate may vary somewhat between career fields; you should become familiar with the standards for your field and dress accordingly (refer back to Chapter Five for more discussion on dress). In addition to your clothing, your posture and facial expressions will also affect how you are perceived. It is important to project confidence and enthusiasm during the interview while not coming across as insincere. The best advice is to be yourself—just be your *best* self!

There are certain questions that an interviewer is not permitted to ask you, except in very particular circumstances. Because federal law prohibits employment discrimination on the basis of sex, race, marital status, age, religion, national origin, and disability status, these matters are only relevant to an employment decision in the event that they have been proven to be job-related (Hamilton & Parker, 1997, p. 259). Hamilton and Parker (1997) give two criteria for evaluating whether an interview question is legal:

> *All questions must be job-related.* The interviewer must be prepared to prove that the questions are related to the specific job.

> *The same basic questions must be asked of all applicants for the position.* In other words, an interviewer cannot have one set of questions for ethnic minorities, another for women, and still another for white males. (p. 259)

Just because some questions are illegal doesn't mean they don't get asked. If you are asked an illegal question, you should be prepared to handle the situation in a professional manner. Think about how you might respond to an illegal question, keeping in mind that antagonizing the interviewer may hurt your chances at getting the job. One way to address the situation without becoming overtly antagonistic is to address the possible concerns behind the question (Hamilton & Parker, 1997, p. 263). For instance, if you are asked whether you have children, you might respond: "If you are worried that I won't be able to meet the time demands of this job, I assure you that I understand what is involved and I am willing to make the appropriate commitment." This addresses a legitimate concern that may be related to the question, but deflects the conversation away from inappropriate topics. Ultimately, you must be prepared to decide whether there are topics that, while they may be illegal to ask about, you are willing to discuss if they come up. And, if you feel strongly about the illegality of certain topics, be prepared to face the potential tension this could cause in an interview should these topics be raised.

Of course, you will want to think about and rehearse answers to the many legal, job-related questions you will be asked. It is likely that you will be asked to elaborate on the job experience described on your resume (including your internship). Wherever possible and ethical, your answers to these questions should highlight how this experience relates to the job you are interviewing for. Many interviewers also ask scenario-driven questions. In these cases, you will be presented with a particular job-related dilemma and asked what you would do if you were ever found yourself in such a situation. Some interviewers will ask you to demonstrate a particular skill on the spot. For example, one of your textbook authors (Cliff) was once asked to persuade the interviewer to buy a tablecloth!

You should also be prepared to answer poorly worded interview questions. Unfortunately, many interviewers lack experience and formal training with job interviewing and so may present you with questions that are inappropriately broad or vague. For example, while interviewing textbooks often warn against it, one of your job interviews will likely begin with the question, "So, tell me about yourself?" Of course, this is actually a difficult question to answer. Where do you begin? Many interviewees struggle to answer this question, so have a plan for how you will answer it. Consider why the question was asked. The question is usually an ill-advised attempt to develop rapport between the interviewer and interviewee, so simply state a few key, interesting, and job-related facts about yourself and keep the answer brief (Hamilton & Parker, 1997).

It may be intimidating to consider all of the questions you could be asked. Fortunately, there are a variety of resources that you may consult as you prepare. Many Web sites offer sample interview questions. We recommend that you consult these as you rehearse for job interviews; the people who actually interview you may consult these as well. Also,

the career placement office on your campus offers interviewing workshops and may conduct mock interviews with students. Finally, your communication department may actually offer a course in which you learn about and practice interviewing. You should consider taking the class even if you do not need it to graduate.

You will also need to arrive at the interview with some questions that you want answered. This is where your early research can come in handy. Organizational Web sites can be a valuable source of information. In addition, it is a good idea to be aware of any news coverage the organization might have had in the recent past. You don't want to ask about a company's overseas operations a month after it liquidated those holdings. Or, you don't want to ask if there is a management-training program if the organization's Web site has an entire link dedicated to explaining just such a program. Also, keep in mind that first interviews are typically not the appropriate time for asking about salary or benefits. These topics are more appropriate for second-round interviews or for after the job has been offered to you.

Negotiating a Job Offer

WHEN YOU GET A JOB OFFER and begin to explore the details of your potential employment, you may have the opportunity (or the need) to negotiate. For your first job there may not be much room to negotiate salary; however, even some entry-level positions have a salary range that varies with qualifications. This is another area where your early research and the work you did establishing realistic goals and expectations can pay off. Hopefully, by the time you get your job offers, you will have some idea of what you are worth on the job market and whether the offers are within an appropriate range. Keep in mind that there are other terms of employment besides salary that you will want to consider before going to work, and some of them

may also be negotiable. For instance, you may want to ask about a flexible work schedule, options for your retirement plan, additional paid vacation, or faster vacation accrual time. Coming out of college, you may also need to negotiate your start date so that it fits with your graduation plans. You may be offered an employment package that is standard and non-negotiable. If so, then you must evaluate the package as it is. But, if you have concerns or are looking for something different than what is first offered to you, it may be worth your time to ask about changes.

Employment Ethics

YOU SHOULD BEGIN PRACTICING employment ethics during the job-search process. During your interviews people will be evaluating your skills, your personality, and your ethics. For instance, speaking badly about former or current employers or colleagues is unprofessional and, if you reveal information that was meant to remain private, it can be unethical as well.

A more complicated situation, and one that may not come up until after you have your first job, involves confidential information (such as client lists). If your job deals with things like client lists, trade secrets, or other specialized business information, your employer will likely have a policy in place to govern what happens to these things if you leave. Playing fast and loose with these policies may seem like a good way to get ahead, but it can have serious ramifications for you and for your new employer if the issue ever comes up in a legal context. Even if you don't get caught up in legal trouble, engaging in behavior such as this can compromise your reputation within your business community.

Another issue that you will probably face at some point is how to look for a new job while you are still working at your current one. The answer to this question will depend on the culture of your current workplace. In some cases, for example, it may be important to look quietly and avoid letting your employer know that you are on the job market. We do not recommend that you intentionally deceive your current employer, but sometimes things can become uncomfortable for you at work if others know you are trying to find a new job.

If you are offered a new job, you should make every effort to ensure that your current employer won't be left in a bind. For instance, giving as much notice of your departure as possible will allow the organization time to prepare. Two weeks' notice is standard, although in some professions a longer notice is expected (for instance, a lawyer leaving a busy litigation firm might give four to six weeks' notice to permit the firm to shift her caseload around). Of course, changing jobs is an imprecise process. You may not be able to time the transition in a way that permits you to give extended notice; this may be unavoidable, but it should not be something you do by design.

Summary

THIS CHAPTER HAS LED YOU through some of the basics of finding a job. Much of the advice is general, and you will need to think about how it might apply to you and to the variety of circumstances in which you will find yourself. So much of job searching, interviewing, and professional life itself is based on your ability to make informed, mature decisions. The better prepared you are, the more you know about the situation you are going into, and the more you have thought about what you are looking for and how you want to get it, the better off you will be.

Review Questions

1. I have my communication degree...now what?

2. What do I need to know about formatting a resume?

3. What sort of research do I need to do before searching for a job?

4. What are the two criteria for determining whether an interview question is legal?

For Further Reading

Garber, J. (2001). *I need a job, now what?* New York: Silver Lining Books.

Graber, S. (2000). *The everything resume book.* Holbrook, MA: Adams Media Corporation.

YOU HAVE NOW REACHED the end of your internship. We know that completing such a challenging endeavor brings many rewards: relief, satisfaction, and hope for your future. We congratulate you on this accomplishment and hope that you have found your internship experience to be a positive one.

Your communication education has provided you with a number of skills and abilities that will serve you well no matter what field you choose to work in. These include conflict-management skills, experience with mentoring and being mentored, group leadership and participation abilities, interpersonal skills, and a critical eye for reading and evaluating arguments. We hope that you have been able to exercise many of these skills as a part of your internship. We also hope that the internship course has given you some new insight into the ways in which you can apply your communication expertise in the working world.

Congratulations on the completion of your internship experience. We wish you the best as you complete your college education and begin the next chapter in your own life.

Altman, I., & Taylor, D. (1973). *Social penetration: The development of interpersonal relationships.* New York: Holt, Rinehart, & Winston.

Bartholomew, K., & Horowitz, L. M. (1991). Attachment styles among young adults: A test of a four-category model. *Journal of Personality and Social Psychology, 61*, 226-244.

Burgoon, J. K., & Hale, J. L. (1988). Nonverbal expectancy violations: Model elaboration and application to immediacy behaviors. *Communication Monographs, 55*, 58-79.

Byrne, D. (1971). *The attraction paradigm.* New York: Academic Press.

Cahn, D. D. (Ed.) (1990). *Intimates in conflict: A communication perspective.* Hillsdale, NJ: Erlbaum.

Canary, D. J., Cupach, W. R., & Messman, S. J. (1995). *Relationship conflict: Conflict in parent-child, friendship, and romantic relationships.* Thousand Oaks, CA: Sage.

Cupach, W. R., & Canary, D. J. (1997). *Competence in interpersonal conflict.* Prospect Heights, IL: Waveland Press.

Floyd, K. (2001). Human affection exchange: I. Reproductive probability as a predictor of men's affection with their sons. *Journal of Men's Studies, 10*, 39-50.

Gross, L. S. (1993). *The internship experience* (2d ed). Prospect Heights, IL: Waveland Press, Inc.

Hamilton, C., & Parker, C. (1997). *Communicating for results: A guide for business & the professions* (5th ed). Belmont, CA: Wadsworth.

Heider, F. (1959). *The psychology of interpersonal relations.* New York: Wiley.

Hocker, J. L., & Wilmot, W. W. (1991). *Interpersonal conflict* (3d ed.). Dubuque, IA: Brown.

Janis, I. L. (1982). *Groupthink.* Boston: Houghton Mifflin.

McCornack, S. A. (1992). Information manipulation theory. *Communication Monographs, 59*, 1-16.

Thourlby, W. (1978). *You are what you wear.* Bardonia, NY: Golden Quill Press.

Witte, K. (1992). Putting the fear back into fear appeals: The extended parallel process model. *Communication Monographs, 59*, 329-349.

Worth, R. (2002). *Webster's new world: Business writing handbook.* Indianapolis: Wiley.

K ORY FLOYD is associate professor, director of graduate MA studies, and former director of internships in the Hugh Downs School of Human Communication at Arizona State University. He holds a PhD in communication from the University of Arizona, an MA in speech communication from the University of Washington, and a BA in English literature from Western Washington University. Dr. Floyd's research focuses on the communication of affection in personal relationships and on the communicative aspects of sibling and parent-child relationships. He has earned a number of awards for his research, including the New Scholar of the Year award from the International Network on Personal Relationships.

M ICHELE HAMMERS is assistant professor of communication at Loyola Marymount University and former internship coordinator in the Hugh Downs School of Human Communication at Arizona State University. She holds a PhD in communication and an MA in humanities from Arizona State University, a Juris Doctor from the University of Texas at Austin, and a BS in business from Boston University. Before beginning her graduate work, Dr. Hammers was a practicing attorney whose work focused on employment and contract litigation. Her academic focus is in rhetoric with particular interests in representations of female professionalism in popular media texts.

C LIFTON SCOTT is assistant professor of communication studies at the University of North Carolina, Charlotte, and former internship coordinator in the Hugh Downs School of Human Communication at Arizona State University. He holds a PhD in communication from Arizona State University, an MA in communication studies from Northern Illinois University, and a BS in speech communication from Bradley University. Dr. Scott's research focuses on organizational communication with particular interests in the communication of professional identity, safety culture, and high-reliability organizing.

Appendix A: Internship Contract

Appendix B: Mentor Midterm Evaluation

Appendix C: Sponsor Application

Appendix D: Time Log

Appendix E: Sample Resumes

Appendix F: Sample Cover Letters

INTERNSHIP CONTRACT

_____

Intern Name _____ Phone _____

WILL COMPLETE a _____ credit internship totaling _____ hours of on-the-job work.

Start date _____ End date _____ Work hours _____

NOTE: This contract is due no later than the <u>first day of classes</u> for each semester.

Employer Organization _____

Mentor _____ Email: _____

Phone _____ FAX: _____

Address _____

_____

My internship responsibilities are <u>specifically related to my communication major</u> in the following ways:

_____

_____

_____

My other job responsibilities will include the following: _____

_____

_____

_____

Are there special concerns the Internship Director should know about? If so, please write them here.

_____

_____

Intern Signature _____ Date_____

Mentor Signature _____ Date_____

Note: This form is to be completed by the intern.

_____

<u>Office use only</u>

____ Contract approved: _Clearly shows application of communication concepts._

____ Contract tentatively approved: _Clarification of applicability needed._   Verified: _____

____ Contract NOT approved: _Not applicable._

MENTOR MIDTERM EVALUATION

_____

Intern Name _____   ID# _____

Sponsoring Organization _____

Address _____

_____

Mentor _____

Phone _____   Email: _____

Please comment briefly, but specifically, about your intern's performance in each of the following areas (feel free to write "N/A" if not applicable). Also, circle a general rating for your intern for each area—whether you feel that your intern's performance was _"poor," "below average," "average," "above average,"_ or _"excellent."_

_____

PROFESSIONAL DEMEANOR/   poor   below average   average   above average   excellent
PUNCTUALITY

COMPETENCE   poor   below average   average   above average   excellent

ABILITY TO WORK WELL WITH   poor   below average   average   above average   excellent
OTHERS

INITIATIVE/ABILITY TO HANDLE ASSIGNMENTS INDEPENDENTLY

poor   below average   average   above average   excellent

ABILITY TO FOLLOW INSTRUCTIONS ACCURATELY

poor   below average   average   above average   excellent

COMMENTS/SUGGESTIONS FOR IMPROVEMENT

PLEASE COMPLETE THE FOLLOWING REGARDING YOUR INTERN:

Overall, I would rate the performance of my intern up to this point in time as (circle one):

poor   below average   average   above average   excellent

Would you like to be contacted to discuss your intern's performance further (circle one)?

not necessary   yes (suggested time/date: _____)

Mentor Signature _____ Date_____

I have met with my sponsor and been informed of my evaluation.

Intern Signature _____ Date_____

SPONSOR APPLICATION

_____

Please check appropriate box: ☐ One-time internship; Intern name _____

Date: _____ ☐ Continuing opportunity

Name of Organization _____

Address: _____

_____

_____

Phone: _____ Fax: _____

Please do not fax this form.

General nature of your organization:

Title of internship position:

Description of internship duties:

Relation of internship to human communication:

Special incentives:

Geographical/logistical limitations:

Number of internships available:

Organizational contact:

Name:

Title:

Phone:

Fax:

Email:

Please attach a
business card
here

TIME LOG

_____

INTERN NAME:

ID #:

SPONSORING AGENCY:

MENTOR:

INTERNSHIP START DATE:

MENTOR REVIEW OF TIME LOG

I have reviewed my intern's work and can verify the hours shown below.

	to be filled out by intern		_to be filled out by mentor_	
	Hours worked	Total hours		
Week	this period	to date	Mentor signature	Date
_____	_____ / _____		_____	_____
_____	_____ / _____		_____	_____
_____	_____ / _____		_____	_____
_____	_____ / _____		_____	_____
_____	_____ / _____		_____	_____
_____	_____ / _____		_____	_____
_____	_____ / _____		_____	_____
_____	_____ / _____		_____	_____
_____	_____ / _____		_____	_____
_____	_____ / _____		_____	_____
_____	_____ / _____		_____	_____
_____	_____ / _____		_____	_____
_____	_____ / _____		_____	_____
_____	_____ / _____		_____	_____
_____	_____ / _____		_____	_____
_____	_____ / _____		_____	_____

UPON COMPLETION OF INTERNSHIP

MENTOR SIGNATURE _____ DATE _____

Diane R. Jacobsen

112 Skyline Drive, Apt. 30

Creighton, ID 82412

Employment Objective

Administrative assistant in a marketing or advertising firm.

Education

Bachelor of Arts in Communication (expected June 2001), University of Idaho. Minor in business management. GPA: 3.92

Associate of Arts, 1999, Creighton Community College.

> Major in communication studies. GPA: 4.0.

Work History

Marketing Intern, D. A. James Marketing, 41 South Street, Creighton, ID 82412. January 2001 to present. Assist marketing manager in the design of promotional campaigns. Buy print advertising for various products. Support account executives in the fulfillment of client needs.

Administrative Assistant, Department of Political Science, University of Idaho, Moscow, ID, 82870. August 1999 to January 2001. Supported the chair and assistant chair of the department. Scheduled appointments and screened all callers. Prepared weekly reports on faculty activities. Advertised departmental events through university media channels.

Desk Clerk, Thomsen Media Service Center, Creighton Community College, Creighton, ID, 82412. September 1997 to May 1999. Checked out movies and videos to professors and teaching assistants. Recorded return dates and sent follow-up reminders. Catalogued all incoming materials. Assisted the director and staff with administrative duties.

Extracurricular Activities and Awards

- Associated Students' Vice President for Marketing, 2000-2001
- Volunteer tutor for developmentally disabled adolescents, 1997-present
- Outstanding Senior, Department of Communication, 2001
- Secretary of Communication Students' Association, 1999-2000

References gladly furnished on request.

Diane R. Jacobsen

112 Skyline Drive, Apt. 30

Creighton, ID 82412

(250) 741-6638

Employment Objective

Administrative assistant in a marketing or advertising firm.

Education

Bachelor of Arts in Communication (expected June 2001), University of Idaho. Minor in business management. GPA: 3.92

Associate of Arts, 1999, Creighton Community College. Major in communication studies. GPA: 4.0.

Work History

Marketing Intern, D. A. James Marketing, 41 South Street, Creighton, ID 82412. January 2001 to present. Assist marketing manager in the design of promotional campaigns. Buy print advertising for various products. Support account executives in the fulfillment of client needs.

Administrative Assistant, Department of Political Science, University of Idaho, Moscow, ID, 82870. August 1999 to January 2001. Supported the chair and assistant chair of the department. Scheduled appointments and screened all callers. Prepared weekly reports on faculty activities. Advertised departmental events through university media channels.

Desk Clerk, Thomsen Media Service Center, Creighton Community College, Creighton, ID, 82412. September 1997 to May 1999. Checked out movies and videos to professors and teaching assistants. Recorded return dates and sent follow-up reminders. Catalogued all incoming materials. Assisted the director and staff with administrative duties.

Extracurricular Activities and Awards

Associated Students' Vice President for Marketing, 2000-2001

Volunteer tutor for developmentally disabled adolescents, 1997-present

Outstanding Senior, Department of Communication, 2001

Secretary of Communication Students' Association, 1999-2000

References

Gladly furnished on request.

Diane R. Jacobsen

112 Skyline Drive, Apt. 30

Creighton, ID 82412

(250) 741-6638

Employment Objective

Administrative assistant in a marketing or advertising firm.

Education

Bachelor of Arts in Communication (expected June 2001), University of Idaho. Minor in business management. GPA: 3.92

Associate of Arts, 1999, Creighton Community College. Major in communication studies. GPA: 4.0.

Work History

Marketing Intern, D. A. James Marketing, 41 South Street, Creighton, ID 82412. January 2001 to present. Assist marketing manager in the design of promotional campaigns. Buy print advertising for various products. Support account executives in the fulfillment of client needs.

Administrative Assistant, Department of Political Science, University of Idaho, Moscow, ID, 82870. August 1999 to January 2001. Supported the chair and assistant chair of the department. Scheduled appointments and screened all callers. Prepared weekly reports on faculty activities. Advertised departmental events through university media channels.

Desk Clerk, Thomsen Media Service Center, Creighton Community College, Creighton, ID, 82412. September 1997 to May 1999. Checked out movies and videos to professors and teaching assistants. Recorded return dates and sent follow-up reminders. Catalogued all incoming materials. Assisted the director and staff with administrative duties.

Extracurricular Activities and Awards

- Associated Students' Vice President for Marketing, 2000-2001

- Volunteer tutor for developmentally disabled adolescents, 1997-present

- Outstanding Senior, Department of Communication, 2001

- Secretary of Communication Students' Association, 1999-2000

References

Gladly furnished on request.

```
Diane R. Jacobsen
112 Skyline Drive, Apt. 30
Creighton, ID 82412
(250) 741-6638
```

Employment Objective

Administrative assistant in a marketing or advertising firm.

Education

Bachelor of Arts in Communication (expected June 2001). University of Idaho.

Minor in business management.

Coursework in: Advertising and marketing.

GPA: 3.92

Associate of Arts (1999). Creighton Community College.

Major in communication studies.

GPA: 4.0.

Work History

Marketing Intern, D. A. James Marketing. 41 South Street, Creighton, ID 82412. (January 2001 to present). Assist marketing manager in the design of promotional campaigns. Buy print advertising for various products. Support account executives in the fulfillment of client needs.

Administrative Assistant, Department of Political Science, University of Idaho. Moscow, ID, 82870. (August 1999 to January 2001). Supported the chair and assistant chair of the department. Scheduled appointments and screened all callers. Prepared weekly reports on faculty activities. Advertised departmental events through university media channels.

Desk Clerk, Thomsen Media Service Center, Creighton Community College. Creighton, ID, 82412. (September 1997 to May 1999). Checked out movies and videos to professors and teaching assistants. Recorded return dates and sent follow-up reminders. Catalogued all incoming materials. Assisted the director and staff with administrative duties.

Extracurricular Activities and Awards

- Associated Students' Vice President for Marketing (2000-2001)
- Volunteer tutor for developmentally disabled adolescents (1997-present)
- Outstanding Senior, Department of Communication (2001)
- Secretary of Communication Students' Association (1999-2000)

References

Gladly furnished on request.

Diane R. Jacobsen

112 Skyline Drive, Apt. 30

Creighton, ID 82412

(250) 741-6638

Employment Objective

Administrative assistant in a marketing or advertising firm.

Education

Bachelor of Arts in Communication (expected June 2001), University of Idaho. Minor in business management. GPA: 3.92

Associate of Arts, 1999, Creighton Community College.

Major in communication studies. GPA: 4.0.

Work History

Marketing Intern   *January 2001 to present*

D. A. James Marketing, 41 South Street, Creighton, ID 82412

Assist marketing manager in the design of promotional campaigns. Buy print advertising for various products. Support account executives in the fulfillment of client needs.

Administrative Assistant   *August 1999 to January 2001*

Department of Political Science, University of Idaho, Moscow, ID, 82870.

Supported the chair and assistant chair of the department. Scheduled appointments and screened all callers. Prepared weekly reports on faculty activities. Advertised departmental events through university media channels.

Desk Clerk, Thomsen Media Service Center   *September 1997 to May 1999*

Creighton Community College, Creighton, ID, 82412.

Checked out movies and videos to professors and teaching assistants. Recorded return dates and sent follow-up reminders. Catalogued all incoming materials. Assisted the director and staff with administrative duties.

Extracurricular Activities and Awards

- Associated Students' Vice President for Marketing, 2000-2001

- Volunteer tutor for developmentally disabled adolescents, 1997-present

- Outstanding Senior, Department of Communication, 2001

- Secretary of Communication Students' Association, 1999-2000

References

Gladly furnished on request.

Diane R. Jacobsen
112 Skyline Drive, Apt. 30
Creighton, ID 82412
(250) 741-6638

Employment Objective

Administrative assistant in a marketing or advertising firm.

Education

Bachelor of Arts in Communication (expected June 2001), University of Idaho. Minor in business management. GPA: 3.92

Associate of Arts, 1999, Creighton Community College. Major in communication studies. GPA: 4.0.

Work History

Marketing Intern, D. A. James Marketing, 41 South Street, Creighton, ID 82412. January 2001 to present. Assist marketing manager in the design of promotional campaigns. Buy print advertising for various products. Support account executives in the fulfillment of client needs.

Administrative Assistant, Department of Political Science, University of Idaho, Moscow, ID, 82870. August 1999 to January 2001. Supported the chair and assistant chair of the department. Scheduled appointments and screened all callers. Prepared weekly reports on faculty activities. Advertised departmental events through university media channels.

Desk Clerk, Thomsen Media Service Center, Creighton Community College, Creighton, ID, 82412. September 1997 to May 1999. Checked out movies and videos to professors and teaching assistants. Recorded return dates and sent follow-up reminders. Catalogued all incoming materials. Assisted the director and staff with administrative duties.

Extracurricular Activities and Awards

- Associated Students' Vice President for Marketing, 2000-2001

- Volunteer tutor for developmentally disabled adolescents, 1997-present

- Outstanding Senior, Department of Communication, 2001

- Secretary of Communication Students' Association, 1999-2000

References

Gladly furnished on request.

112 Skyline Drive, Apt. 30
Creighton, ID 82412

June 1, 2005

Mr. George Pearson
Director of Personnel
Olympic Advertising
PO Box 749
Phoenix, AZ 85280

Dear Mr. Pearson:

Please accept this letter as my application for your administrative assistant position, which you recently advertised in the *Arizona Republic*.

You will notice on my enclosed resume that I have a good deal of experience in the advertising field. I will be graduating in two weeks with a Bachelor of Arts in Communication and have taken several courses in advertising and marketing. I have also recently completed a 16-week internship at D. A. James Marketing in Creighton, ID. During my internship, I was responsible for working on a number of marketing campaigns and coordinating with several advertising firms in the area.

In addition to my background in advertising and marketing, I would also bring to this position a strong set of administrative skills. I have completed a college minor in business management and have developed my skills in scheduling, public interface, report writing, and office admini-stration during my work with the Department of Political Science at the University of Idaho. I am confident that these administrative skills, along with my education and background in ad-vertising, make me a strong candidate for this position.

Thank you for considering my application. I will look forward to hearing from you soon.

Sincerely yours,

Diane R. Jacobsen

Enclosure

4500 Belford Ave., Apt. 8A
Westchester, CA 90040
317-410-0525

June 1, 2005

Ms. Sara James
Galaxy Promotions & Events
8600 Washington Blvd.
Culver City, CA 90000

Dear Ms. James:

I am writing to apply for the promotion department internship position that you recently announced through my university's internship office. I have enclosed my resume and at this time wish to highlight a few of my qualifications for the position as you described it.

As I complete my undergraduate degree in Communication Studies, I am seeking opportunities to gain hands-on experience in the field of marketing and product promotion. My education includes courses in small group communication and organizational leadership, and I have extensive experience working with teams of people to accomplish both short- and long-term projects. In addition, I have taken courses in marketing and am familiar with basic product promotion strategies.

While attending college, I have worked as an office assistant in different professional environments; as a result, I have developed strong office skills, including a familiarity with Microsoft Word, Excel, and PowerPoint. In addition to my office skills, I also have experience writing press releases, formal correspondence, and internal memoranda. I am confident that the combination of my education and work experience makes me a strong candidate for your internship position.

Thank you for considering my application. I look forward to an opportunity to discuss my qualifications with you in the near future.

Very truly yours,

Matthew Brewster

Enclosure